THE HEART OF THE SALE

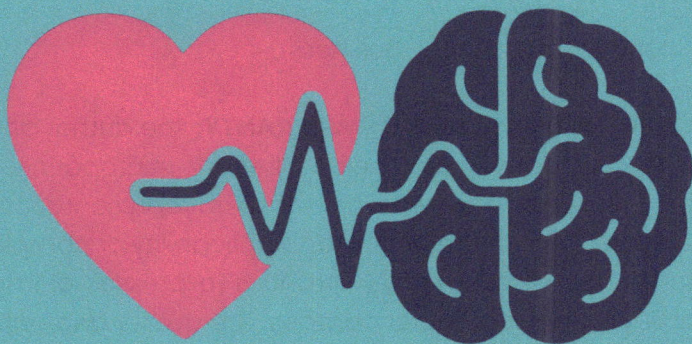

7 STEPS TO EMBRACE THE ART OF SERVING OVER SELLING

MARCUS ELWELL

Author: Marcus Elwell

Title: The Heart of The Sale Book

ISBN: 978-1-917815-07-9

Category: Motivational / Sales / Business

Dedication

To my incredible family and friends this book
is dedicated to you all.

My anchor in the storms, my cheerleaders in
the climb, and my safe place to land.

Your love, loyalty, and unwavering belief in
me have been the foundation beneath every
step forward.

This is as much yours as it is mine.

FOREWORD

Over the past two decades, I've had the privilege of working with thousands of speakers, coaches, and business owners - helping them transform their communication skills and ultimately win more clients. I've seen firsthand how powerful it can be when someone learns to present with clarity, conviction, and true service in mind. Because when you speak to sell, you're not just sharing information - you're shifting beliefs and inspiring action. And that's precisely why I was immediately struck by Marcus Elwell.

Marcus attended one of my 4-day Public Speakers University events, and I remember thinking, "There's something different about this one." You get used to picking up on people who have that spark - that rare mix of empathy, insight, and presence that can hold a room or a conversation with equal weight. Marcus had it. Still does. But more than that, he had a heart for what truly matters in business: connection and service.

It wasn't long before we found ourselves working together. And now, we co-lead The Heart of The Sale University and Academy, where we teach a framework that flips the tired old script of pressure-based selling and replaces it with something far more powerful - and far more human.

That framework is captured beautifully in the book you're holding.

Now, before you dive in, let me say this: there are a lot of books on sales. I know - I've read many of them. Some are filled with techniques that feel a bit outdated... or frankly, manipulative. The kind of stuff that has given "sales" a bad name. Pushy scripts, objection smashing, assumptive closes - the list goes on.

But Marcus's approach? It's something else entirely.

The Heart of The Sale doesn't just teach you how to sell - it teaches you how to serve. That one distinction changes everything. And yet, it's not fluff. Marcus has created a seven-step process that's as practical as it is principled. It doesn't just help you close more sales (though it absolutely will). It helps you build lasting relationships, deepen trust, and position yourself as a true partner to your clients.

Which, if you ask me, is exactly what today's buyers want.

Gone are the days when you could pressure someone into a yes. Today, people want to feel understood. They want to know you're in their corner — not just trying to hit your quota. And that's where Marcus excels. He teaches how to bring humanity back into the process. He shows you how to elevate your mindset from "What can I get?" to "How can I help?" And he proves — with real stories and actionable tools — that this shift doesn't cost you the sale. It creates it.

In fact, it's the same philosophy that underpins the work I've done for over 20 years. Whether I'm helping a business leader design a keynote, a coach craft a webinar, or a company drive conversions through storytelling — the goal has always been the same: communicate with care, clarity, and purpose. Because when you speak from the heart, people listen. And more importantly, they trust you. That's what Marcus has captured here.

This book is a handbook for anyone tired of being "salesy," anyone who's great at what they do but hates the idea of pushing people, and anyone who knows deep down that selling doesn't have to feel uncomfortable — for you or the person you're speaking with.

And here's the best bit: the ideas in this book don't just make you a better salesperson. They make you a better communicator. A better business owner. A better leader.

Because when you sell with heart, you lead with integrity. And people feel that.

So, as you turn the page, I encourage you to keep an open mind — and an open heart. You'll discover frameworks that you can implement right away. But more importantly, you'll discover a philosophy of selling that's built to last.

Marcus Elwell is the real deal. Not just because he's mastered the art of sales — but because he understands what really matters: people.

And The Heart of The Sale is his gift to them — and to you.

Enjoy the read.

Andy Harrington
Founder, Professional Speakers Academy
Creator of Speakers University and The Professional Speakers Academy
Co-Creator of The Heart of The Sale University.

Winning my award for best in sales

CONTENTS

INTRODUCTION

Would you like to experience more sales in your business - the right kind of sales? The kind of sales where you're consistently attracting your tribe... Where every interaction feels aligned, joyful, and easy...

Where results flow in like clockwork, not chaos.

Sounds good, right?

But maybe here's where you are right now:

You're a passionate, purpose-driven business owner. You've got a solid offer, a genuine heart for helping others, and a dream that won't quit. But when it comes to sales? You freeze. Not because you're lazy or unmotivated—no, you're anything but. It's just that the way sales is traditionally taught... it doesn't feel like you. It feels inauthentic, forced, even icky. Sure, you've landed a few clients through referrals or your small circle. Maybe you've dabbled in social media - Instagram, LinkedIn, a YouTube video or two. You've attended events, joined panels, maybe even hosted a masterclass. You've done the 'visibility thing,' and yet, it's like you're throwing spaghetti at the wall hoping something sticks. But it's not sticking. And it's starting to feel personal. You delay. You second-guess. You tell yourself you'll figure it out tomorrow - but tomorrow keeps ghosting you like a bad lead. You've had Zoom calls that felt hopeful... until they ended with a polite "I'll think about it." You give, and give, and give - offering incredible value - but still hear:

"I need to ask my partner,"
"I can't afford it,"
"I'll circle back."

And then... nothing.

It hurts. It's draining. And it chips away at your confidence every single time. Maybe, in those moments, you start wondering:

"Is it me? Is my offer not as good as I thought?"

"Why do others seem to close with ease, while I feel like I'm tap-dancing for free?"

Let's be real: you're not in business to be a motivational speaker who gets ghosted. You're here to transform lives - and that transformation starts with a "Yes." But getting that yes shouldn't require pushy tactics, high-pressure closes, or becoming someone you're not.

What if every sales conversation could feel like genuine service - not sales at all?

What if your dream clients leaned in, lit up, and said:
"This is exactly what I need. When can we start?"
No awkward close. No discounting. No convincing.
Just clarity. Confidence. Conversion.
That's exactly what *The Heart of the Sale is about.*

This book isn't just another sales script. It's a movement. A method.
A moment in time where the authentic seller finally wins.

The Heart of the Sale system is a framework designed for entrepreneurs who want to sell without selling out. It guides you through clear, proven phases that help your client uncover their truth and say yes - without you ever needing to push or pitch.

Here's why it works:

1. **You'll never wing it again:** You'll know exactly what to ask and when.
2. **You'll stop dreading objections:** Because your client does the convincing.
3. **It works across all industries:** Coaching, consulting, services - this system adapts.
4. **It's real. It's human. It's authentic:** Because your success doesn't come from hard-sell tactics, but from heart-led conversations.

Why now?

Because we're living in a trust recession.

People are sceptical. Between misinformation, economic fear, and the explosion of AI, most buyers are on high alert. They don't know who to trust - and they certainly don't want to be sold to.

Your competitors are catching on. They're learning how to have these authentic, connected conversations. If you don't embrace a new way of selling, they'll win the yes instead of you.

Let's also be honest - we're not getting any younger. Every "maybe" you hear that doesn't convert is time and impact lost. Every unclosed deal is a client still stuck in their problem and transformation delayed.

It's time to stop hoping for the sale and start leading it - with heart. Welcome to The Heart of the Sale.

Let's reclaim what selling was always meant to be: service, done right. So Let Me Ask You...

What if, instead of all this hustle, things actually started to click? Imagine it's Tuesday at 3PM. You've just finished your third call of the day, and two of them converted. You've made money, served your people, and feel energised and empowered.

Now it's Friday evening. You're looking at your diary for next week, it's full of aligned potential clients who found you through your new framework. You're no longer guessing or hoping, you have a system. You know your numbers, and you know next week will bring even more results.

Imagine stepping on stage at a packed event. The room hums with energy.

You're introduced as the expert. You're confident. You're credible. You deliver with authenticity, and people are lining up to connect with you, to thank you, and most importantly... to work with you.

And picture this: you're on holiday. Paid in full. You're sipping wine in the sun, knowing business is thriving without you needing to push. Why? Because you've built a system. You're no longer relying on chance. You're in control. You're in flow.

So How Do You Get There?

With a **Heart-Centred Sales Approach.**

This isn't about manipulation or pressure. It's about understanding your buyer deeply. Asking powerful questions. Creating connection. Selling in a way that feels **good** - for *you* and *them*.

Because when you care more about the person's result than the money - everyone wins.

This is **not** fluffy. It's a proven system. And it's working *right now* for people just like you - solo entrepreneurs, growing teams, even seven-figure businesses.

So, the question is how much longer are you going to wait, because the more opportunity you leave on the table, the harder it gets. You're not getting any younger. The people who need you aren't finding you. You deserve to feel confident, in control, and prosperous in your business - not stuck, stressed, or second-guessing.

A heart-centred approach helps you:

Serve your clients better

Sell without sleaze

Stand out in your industry

Build long-term, trusted relationships

And ultimately... make more impact and income

Why Listen to Me?

For over 20 years, I've built and scaled multiple businesses - from zero to seven figures - not just chasing numbers, but creating real, sustainable profit. I've taken this same sales approach into dozens of other businesses and helped entrepreneurs like you go from stuck to soaring - from £0 to £10k, £50k, £100k months and beyond.

This isn't theory. It's field-tested.

My journey began as an 18-year-old with no clue about retail, standing in a bathroom tile shop, face-to-face with my first potential customer. I had no experience, but I had heart. I asked the right questions. I listened. I served. And I made the sale.

That one moment shaped everything. I realised sales isn't about convincing — it's about connecting.

And Here's the Truth:

No one likes being *sold to*. But we all love to buy.

When you learn to lead conversations from the heart, you never have to "sell" again.

You simply invite people to take the next natural step.

That's real sales success.

Not just closing a sale - but opening a relationship

"Real success doesn't come from closing a deal it comes from opening a relationship."

What if the key to attracting consistent sales, loyal clients, and real business growth wasn't about pressure, tactics, or hustle? What if the secret was far simpler, more human, and more sustainable? What if it started with this:

Serve first!

That's the heart of this book, and the foundation of everything I believe about authentic selling. *The Heart of The Sale* is not just another sales manual. It's a philosophy. A movement. A mindset shift that allows entrepreneurs, leaders, and everyday business owners to approach selling in a way that feels aligned, fulfilling, and deeply effective.

This isn't just another sales book. It's a personal and professional journey. Born from my own transformation, through crisis, entrepreneurship, and rebuilding from rock bottom, I've learned that the most powerful sales tool isn't a pitch. It's presence. It's empathy. It's listening with your heart and leading with intention.

As a young entrepreneur at 18, I built my first business from scratch. By 39, I had multiple businesses and a life that looked successful from the outside. But behind the scenes, I was facing personal heartbreak, financial uncertainty, and a battle for my health that would redefine everything I believed about success. Surviving a brain tumour gave me clarity. I could no longer ignore the fact that life is too short to sell in a way that doesn't feel right.

So, I rewired my mindset. I reimagined the sales process. I rebuilt myself and my business, on a foundation of service over selling.

That experience taught me that success isn't about chasing the next sale. It's about who you become in the process of serving others. It's about showing up, heart first. It's about turning strangers into clients, and clients into lifelong champions - through trust, not tricks.

For many entrepreneurs, the very word "sales" brings discomfort. Maybe that's you. Maybe you've tried scripts that didn't feel like you, followed advice that felt pushy, or signed up for programs that promised quick wins but left you more confused and disconnected. Maybe you've sat at your desk, full of potential, but paralysed by the fear of rejection or failure.

I get it. I've been there.

But I want to offer you a different path, a path that feels good and gets results. A path rooted in empathy, curiosity, and service. Because when you sell with sincerity, you don't just make a sale - you make an impact. You create real transformation in the lives of your clients. And in turn, your business becomes something far more meaningful than just a transaction engine. It becomes a force for good.

The Heart of The Sale is your invitation to step into that version of yourself, the business owner who doesn't sell out their values to grow. The entrepreneur who turns conversations into conversions because they lead with care. The human being who knows that selling isn't about taking, it's about giving first and trusting that what you give will always come back multiplied.

So, if you're holding this book, it's probably not by accident.

You're here because something inside you knows there's more to your business, your purpose, and YOU. You're not just looking for more clients – you're looking for more *connection, more meaning,* and a way to grow a business that reflects the truth of who you are. You're tired of pretending, pushing, and performing. You want results, yes, but not at the expense of your soul.

Wherever you are in your journey – just starting out, rebuilding, or looking to scale with more soul – I want to remind you: you don't need to become someone else to succeed. You just need to return to your heart. Because that's where the real power is.

And when you lead with that?

Everybody Wins.

"Turn strangers into clients, and clients into lifelong champions through trust, not tricks"

CHAPTER ONE

FROM THE SAHARA TO THE SELF

A journey of healing, purpose, and heart-led sales

I'm sitting atop a golden sand dune in the heart of the Sahara Desert. The sun is slowly retreating behind a jagged mountain range, painting the sky in brushstrokes of deep orange and soft violet. It's around 6:20 in the evening. The air is still, sacred almost - the kind of silence that makes you stop and hear things you've buried for far too long. Only the wind dares to whisper, gliding across the sand like a memory too sacred to speak out loud. Thousands of miles away from home, I sit here at the start of a soul-stirring trek, a journey born from both pain and purpose, all in support of brain tumour research, a cause forever etched into the fabric of who I am.

And in that moment - on that dune, under that burning sky - the past rises in me like a tide. I begin to remember.

I remember the weight of the diagnosis.

The blur of hospital corridors.

The sterile smell of fear.

The surgeon's voice as calm as it was terrifying.

The prayer I whispered when I didn't know if I'd ever wake up again. Because you see, just four years earlier, my head, this very head that now holds dreams, vision, and fierce determination, was opened not to end my life, but to save it.

A brain tumour.

Four years before my surgery, I had lost my beloved Uncle Peter to the same ruthless disease. He didn't get the miracle I did. And I carry that with me every single day. His absence left a void, yes, but it also lit a fire. A fire that says: *"This is not how the story ends."*

Since that day, I've made a vow. A vow to speak, to walk, to raise funds, to raise hope, to raise awareness - because we must do better.

In a country as rich and resourced as the UK - the fifth-largest economy in the world - only 15% of those diagnosed with a cancerous brain tumour will live beyond five years. That number is not just a statistic. It's someone's daughter. Someone's father. Someone's best friend. It was almost me.

That is unacceptable.

It must change.

So, as I sit here, not just in the desert, but in deep reflection, I realise something profound. Survival is not the end of the story. It's the beginning of responsibility. The responsibility to stand in the gap. To speak for those who no longer can. To fight, not just for life, but for the quality and dignity of it.

This chapter of my life didn't start in the Sahara. It started in a hospital bed. And yet here I am, under the vastness of an African sky, reminded that healing isn't just about what the body survives, it's about what the soul chooses to do after.

And I choose purpose. I choose legacy.

I choose to walk - for the ones who can't.

And to speak - for the ones whose voices were silenced too soon.

Surviving the storm was just the beginning. What came next was the quiet, relentless work of becoming, peeling back the layers of fear, guilt, and uncertainty to rediscover the man underneath. In this book we will navigate from physical survival to emotional and spiritual resilience that led me to the path of sales – selling from the heart. I'll walk you through the mindset shifts that not only shaped my recovery, but also the moments that forced me to choose faith over fear, and the power

I found in finally owning and speaking my story. Because true healing doesn't just come from what we overcome, it comes from how we rise and use that pain to empower others. This is where transformation begins. This is where the voice you once silenced becomes your greatest tool. And this is where we learn that resilience isn't about bouncing back, it's about rising different, stronger, and more aligned with purpose.

This is where the journey inward begins.

This isn't just my journey.

It's ours.

And that's why I'm here. That's what brought me to this vast, sacred land of sand, silence, and stars.

We've just completed our first 10km trek after two days of travel - planes, buses, and finally, our feet. It's been nine hours on foot, punctuated by brief pit stops. And now, at this moment, I'm overwhelmed with gratitude. I'm alive. I'm breathing. I get to be here. I get to witness this sunset. I get to feel the enormity of life and the fragility of it too. Around me, the dunes stretch endlessly, sprinkled with unexpected pockets of greenery - far lusher than I imagined the Sahara would be.

Tonight, we have the choice to sleep in a tent or under the stars by the fire. Our guides gentle, peaceful people have told us there's no moon visible this week due to the Earth's position. That means the stars will shine even brighter. I've chosen the stars. I want to lie there and soak in the silence, to be completely present. To feel the universe above me and the earth beneath me. To be thankful for my second chance.

The Building Years: Brick by Brick, Belief by Belief

Let me take you back, not just before the tumour, but to a time when life seemed certain, or at least, controllable.
I was 18 years old when I first tasted what it meant to build something of my own. It was the year 2000, and while most of my peers were figuring out what university courses to take or where the next party was, I was in the trenches of real-world entrepreneurship. I co-founded a retail business with my father. A family dream, built with bare hands, blind faith, and bold ambition. Eighteen months later, my older brother joined us, and the business grew.

But let's pause here, because it's easy to skim over this part.

Eighteen. Years. Old.

Still a teenager but holding responsibilities far beyond my age. I didn't have the luxury of ease or certainty. I had to learn quickly that if I wanted to create a future, I had to build it myself. That required a mindset far more mature than the years I had lived.

Entrepreneurship at that age isn't just about business. It's about belief, the kind you must fiercely protect even when no one claps for you. You must be self-led, self-fed, and self-aware. You're not just selling products or services, you're developing grit. You're navigating doubt, rejection, comparison, and failure, all while your peers are still being spoon-fed direction. You learn to be your own compass.

And through those early years, I adopted a mindset that would serve me well... and sometimes, serve me too well. One that said: Work hard. Be strong. *Don't quit. Keep building.*

Fast forward two decades, and I was living the results of that mindset. At 39, I had built multiple businesses. I was thriving in property. From the outside, it looked like I had "made it." The accolades, the titles, the business cards — they all said *success*.

But here's what they didn't say:
They didn't say how much I was grieving.
They didn't show the cracks in my foundation.

I had recently gone through a painful breakup with the mother of my three children, a heartbreak that left more than just emotional bruises. Then COVID-19 came and swept through like a storm, shaking every system we had come to rely on. My finances were volatile. My faith in myself even more so.

But the deepest wound?
I had fallen out of love with *me*.

It's the kind of exhaustion that no nap can fix. The kind of emptiness that clings to your bones. I had given so much of myself, to business, to fatherhood, to community, to others, that somewhere along the way, I stopped seeing my own worth. I stopped seeing the man behind the mission. The boy who once dreamed big at 18 had grown into a man who couldn't see tomorrow.

That's the dangerous thing about being a high-functioning visionary. You can still look successful... while silently falling apart.

And I was. I wanted out. Out of the pressure. Out of the pain. Out of the performance.

But here's the thing I now know:

Sometimes, the breakdown is permission for a breakthrough.
Sometimes, the dream must shatter so you can rebuild it with you at the centre - not the version of you the world applauds, but the one your soul recognises.

In the chapters ahead, I'll take you through how I began the slow work of re-learning my value, re-aligning my purpose, and re-imagining what success really means. But for now, know this:

Your life can look like it's working on paper and still be falling apart in spirit

And sometimes, it's in that raw, unfiltered, humbling space...
that your real story begins.

That moment of despair?
It became my reckoning.
And slowly... my reawakening.

You see, pain has a strange way of cracking you open. Of pulling back the layers you built to protect yourself and revealing the truth underneath. And for me, the truth was this: I didn't want to just survive the storm. I wanted to rebuild differently. I wanted to rise, not back to who I used to be, but toward who I was always meant to become.

So, I began the journey inward. A journey of healing. Of personal development. Because deep down, I knew - I knew - I couldn't be the only one. Surely, I wasn't the first man to face heartbreak. Or loss. Or illness. Or regret. Others had come through it... and so could I. I just needed to learn how.

The world had taught me to look outward, for validation, for distraction, for escape. But healing whispered something different. It invited me inward. No more numbing the pain with alcohol or overwork. No more pretending I was fine when I was falling apart. Instead, I turned to wisdom, books, mentors, voices that spoke life into broken places. I devoured the words of Tony Robbins, Jim Rohn, and biographies of those who had built greatness from ashes. And do you know what stood out most?

Every one of them had cultivated a rhythm of intentional living.

Stillness. Movement. Breathwork. Cold showers. Prayer. Visualisation. They weren't just reacting to life; they were designing it. From the inside out.

So, I did the same.

I just knew I had to get a skillset

I started small. No phone in the first or last 10 minutes of the day. That alone gave me breathing room, space to feel, space to think, space to be. I made space for silence before the noise.

Even here, in the heart of the Sahara, where the sand speaks louder than words and the wind carry ancient whispers, I wake early. I rise before the sun and return to my breath. To my God. To myself.

This morning, as the first light painted the dunes gold, I heard the call to prayer stretch out across the desert like a sacred thread. And in that moment, I realised... I wasn't just healing.

I was meeting a version of myself I had never known before.
Not the man who had built businesses.

Not the man who had worn masks to be what the world needed.
But the real man - quiet, grounded, whole.

And the key to that transformation wasn't a dramatic overhaul.
It was the **little things.**

The small, consistent, daily decisions that seem insignificant but stack up to become everything.

That's how we change. That's how we grow.

1% at a time.

Whether you're an entrepreneur, a parent, or simply a human navigating the mess and beauty of life... it begins with how you show up for you. Speak kindly to yourself. Set your intention. Visualise your day before it begins.

Ask yourself, how do I want to feel? How do I want to love? How do I want to lead?

Because when you practise this daily, confidence begins to rise. Not arrogance. Not ego.

But grounded, quiet confidence, the kind that makes you unshakable.

And that confidence - It changes how you show up in business. In life. In conversations.

Especially when it comes to selling.

Because let's be honest, most of us love to buy. But we hate to sell. Why?

Because we've been taught to sell in ways that feel forced, awkward, and frankly, out of alignment.

But what if I told you... there's another way?

Let's explore it together.

The Heart of The Sale

So many of us love buying, but we hate selling. Why? Because the way we've been taught to sell feels manipulative, awkward, even sleazy. But what if I told you there's another way?

It's not about scripts or closing tactics. It's about connection. It's about asking the right questions. It's about truly understanding someone's needs and desires and guiding them toward a solution if it's the right fit. Not because you want to sell, but because you care.

Think of the best salesperson you ever met. Chances are, they didn't push. They listened. They made you feel heard and valued. That's what heart-led selling is about. It's not about closing a sale. It's about opening a relationship. So many entrepreneurs today are stuck. They're going to events, sending emails, posting online, and getting no traction. They're discouraged. They're watching "gurus" preach tactics that don't align with their values. They're tired of chasing. They're thinking of giving up.

Maybe that's where you are right now.

But imagine a different reality...

It's Monday morning. You wake up early. You feel calm, centred, prepared. You've done your morning practice. You pick up the phone with confidence, not fear. You've got a system in place. A framework that feels right. And it's working. You've got leads. You've got momentum. You've got results.

Six months from now, your calendar is full. Your inbox has inquiries. You're doing webinars, content, and conversations that convert. And you're not faking it. You're not manipulating anyone. You're showing up with heart. With truth. With a story that resonates.

Because that story, the one you've lived, is your superpower.

It's time to bring your story, your skills, and your service together.

And if you're thinking, "But who am I to sell?" let me tell you: you're exactly the person someone else needs to hear from.

And that's what the next chapter is all about.

When I talk about The Heart of The Sale, I'm not talking about a tactic, a script, or some clever way to close deals. I'm talking about a completely different lens through which to view the entire sales process, one that prioritises humanity over hustle, relationships over revenue, and service over self-interest.

The heart of the sale is about leading with empathy.

It's about genuinely caring about the person in front of you, not just what they can do for your bottom line, but who they are, what they're going through, and how you can help make their life better. It means taking the time to listen, not to reply, but to truly understand. It means asking meaningful questions, not to manipulate, but to support. It means seeing sales not as a transaction, but as a transformation, for both you and your client.

At the heart of the sale is connection.

And connection can't be faked. You can't fake care, presence, or authenticity, not for long. People can feel it. They know when you're just trying to "close" them, and they know when you're genuinely interested in helping them make the right decision. And here's the kicker, people want to buy. They just don't want to be sold to. The heart of the sale honours that. It invites people in rather than corners them. It builds trust rather than pressure.

And trust - That's your most valuable currency.

The Heart of the Sale also means understanding that your success is directly tied to how well you serve, not how fast you pitch, not how many cold DMs you send. But how deeply you understand your clients' needs, how thoughtfully you show up, and how consistently you deliver on your promise.

When you sell from the heart, something beautiful happens sales become a byproduct of service.

You stop chasing clients and start attracting them. You stop selling products and start delivering solutions. You stop trying to "win" in the traditional sense and instead create wins for everyone involved, your clients, your business, and most importantly, yourself. Because when you operate from the heart, you don't have to compromise who you are to achieve success. You just have to become more of who you really are.

That is the Heart of The Sale. And that's what this book will show you how to embrace, step by step, story by story, sale by meaningful sale. And so now, let's deepen that understanding, because when you truly grasp those sales is a relationship, a conversation, a commitment to serve, you begin to strip away the layers of fear and discomfort around the idea of "selling."

The fear of rejection.

The fear of judgment.

The fear that you're being "too much" or not enough.

But here's the truth: when you sell from the heart, you are not taking, you are *offering*. You are offering transformation. You are offering answers. You are offering the possibility of something better.

Sales isn't about forcing. It's about *facilitating*.

It's not about pitching. It's about *positioning*.

Not about pressure. But about *presence*.

When you are fully present in the moment, when you truly see and hear the person in front of you, whether that's on a sales call, on stage, in a conversation, you shift the energy. You stop selling in the traditional sense and start guiding, mentoring, serving.

But here's the clincher: you cannot guide someone else to their breakthrough if you're still hiding from your own. You must step into full alignment with who you are, what you carry, and why it matters. That means doing the deep work, unlearning the noise of old stories, shaking off the label's others placed on you, and deciding once and for all that you get to choose how you show up in the world.

I wasn't always comfortable with the idea of sales. In fact, like so many people, the very word used to make me tense up. It felt cold, transactional, even manipulative. And yet, deep down, I knew I had something to offer the world. I just didn't want to become 'that guy' to get it out there. So, I had a decision to make, give up on the impact I wanted to make or find a different way. That decision led me to what I now call *the Heart of The Sale*.

But what do I mean by that?

When I talk about the heart of the sale, I'm talking about a radically different approach, one rooted in service, empathy, and authentic connection. The heart of the sale is about putting people before profits. It's about listening to understand, not just to respond. It's about asking questions not to lead someone into a funnel, but to guide them into a solution that truly serves their needs. You see, people want to buy, they just don't want to be sold to. And that's the distinction most entrepreneurs miss. Selling from the heart isn't about pushing. It's about permission. It's about creating such a safe, aligned, and respectful space that people feel drawn to work with you, not pressured. The heart of the sale is about transformation, not transaction and when you shift from "How can I sell this?" to "How can I serve this person powerfully?" everything changes. You build trust. You build loyalty. You build a business that feels like an extension of your values, not a betrayal of them.

That's what I learned, often the hard way.

I was once stuck in that painful middle ground: full of passion but paralysed by the thought of "selling." I had a business idea. I had experience. I even had people telling me I was good at what I did. But when it came time to promote myself, I froze. I doubted myself. Who was I to charge money for something that came naturally to me? Who was I to speak up?

So, I kept quiet.

I watched as others, less experienced, but more confident, signed clients, got referrals, and expanded their businesses. I cheered them on, but I couldn't help feeling stuck. And I blamed myself. Maybe I just wasn't cut out for this. But here's the truth, I wasn't broken. I was just trying to follow a system that didn't fit me. I didn't want to "close" people. I wanted to open them, open their ideas, their hearts, and their readiness for transformation. That desire led me to study a different path - servant leadership, emotional intelligence, communication, and the psychology of buying. Slowly but surely, I built a new framework for sales. One that felt good. One that worked. One that served people deeply.

And that framework is what this book is about.

In the chapters ahead, I will walk you through seven core steps that will help you embrace the art of serving to sell effectively. Whether you're a seasoned entrepreneur or just starting out, this journey will change the way you see your business, your customers, and yourself. Because when you lead with service, build with heart, and stay aligned with your values, there's no limit to what you can achieve.

And most importantly, *everybody wins.*

it made me dig deeper & reflect on how I'd sever all my life without being consiously aware - when I did get consiously aware I realised I'd always served from the heart which led me to this book.

In the Sahara where I started writing this book.

marcus elwell

SALES MINDSET TRANSFORMATION

Why not connect with me on Facebook as you learn more about The Heart of The Sales

**marcus
elwell**

SALES MINDSET TRANSFORMATION

CHAPTER TWO

MIND OVER MATTER

Cultivating a Service-Oriented Mindset

Success in sales doesn't start with strategy, it starts with mindset. You can have all the scripts, systems, and techniques in the world, but if your internal world isn't aligned with service, consistency, and confidence, the external results will never follow. Sales, at its core, is not about pushing products, it's about helping people. And that starts with how you manage your thoughts, your energy, your emotions, and ultimately, your purpose. Before we dive into methods and mechanics, we need to begin with what's going on inside. Because if you don't believe in yourself, your service, and the value you bring to the table, how can you expect anyone else to? The battle is won or lost in the mind long before you ever pick up the phone or step into a meeting.

Cultivating a service-oriented mindset means shifting from fear to faith. From doubt to determination. From scarcity to generosity. It's about moving from "How do I close this sale?" to "How can I serve this person powerfully, even if they don't buy today?" When you do that, the game changes. You stop chasing clients, and you start attracting the right ones.

In this chapter, we're going to explore how to manage your mind like a master, because the mind is your greatest asset. I'll show you how to inspire and rewire your thinking patterns, navigate hurdles with clarity, and also how to develop and dream again, even after setbacks. We'll also break down the power of systems and routines, because mindset without structure is just good intentions. Together, these tools will help you build a resilient, service-first mentality that sets the foundation for lasting impact and success.

It's not just about selling more, it's about showing up differently.

Let's begin.

Management: Lead Your Mind Before You Lead a Business

When people hear the word management, they often think of spreadsheets, teams, or time tracking. But the first, and most critical, thing you must learn to manage is yourself. Your mindset. Your energy. Your thoughts. Your focus.

Entrepreneurs often jump straight into building offers, creating marketing campaigns, or designing websites. But the truth is, none of that will matter if you're mentally scattered, emotionally drained, or spiritually disconnected. Sustainable success starts from the inside out. Managing your mind is about developing mental leadership. You must become the CEO of your inner world. That means choosing your thoughts as intentionally as you choose your clients. It means checking in with yourself every morning and asking, "What energy am I bringing into today? Am I leading from fear or from service?"

When you adopt a service-oriented mindset, you stop getting stuck in comparison and scarcity. You stop panicking about whether people will say "yes." Instead, you focus on how you can show up powerfully and why your work matters. You remind yourself: "This isn't about me. It's about who I'm here to serve."

That shift alone can transform your day.

Daily management also involves setting boundaries, mental, emotional, and physical. It's choosing not to start your day by scrolling social media or checking emails in a panic. It's giving yourself space in the morning to get grounded and intentional before stepping into action. It's noticing your triggers and creating rituals to bring yourself back into alignment. Your mind is like a garden. If you don't intentionally plant empowering beliefs, weeds of doubt and fear will grow by default. Management is how you tend the soil. It's how you create the conditions for confidence, clarity, and compassion to flourish, not just in your life, but in every interaction, you have with clients.

Remember: how you manage yourself is how you model leadership to others. And leadership rooted in service is what will set you apart. The aim then is to inspire and rewire your mind so that it works for you, not against you.

If management is about taking responsibility for your mindset, inspiration and rewiring is about actively reshaping it.

Here's the truth; the brain is not fixed. It's wired through repetition, belief, and emotion. That means your mindset is not your identity. It's your habit. And habits can be changed.

For many entrepreneurs, especially those who are heart-led and service-driven, there's often a hidden inner script that says things like:

"I'm not good at sales."

"I don't want to come across as pushy."

"People won't pay me that much."

"I need more experience before I can really succeed."

These beliefs feel like facts, but they're not. They're conditioned thoughts, formed from past experiences, family influences, social pressures, and fear-based stories. And unless you challenge them, they run the show. Quietly. Constantly. Holding you back.

To rewire your mindset, you must inspire yourself daily with new, empowering input. This is where affirmations, visualisation, and aligned action come into play not as fluffy self-help trends, but as neural. To rewire your mindset, you must inspire yourself daily with new, empowering input. This is where affirmations, visualisation, and aligned action come into play, not as fluffy self-help trends, but as neural training tools. Every time you choose a belief rooted in service, abundance, and value over one grounded in fear or scarcity, you're building a new mental pathway. You're literally changing the architecture of your brain.

For example, when you choose to see sales as an opportunity to help, rather than a burden to push, you activate a sense of purpose, which inspires energy. When you affirm "My work changes lives" or "I guide people to their best decisions," you're rewiring your perception of your role in the sales process. And when you consistently take small, courageous steps from this new place, like reaching out to serve, following up with care, or asking deeper questions, you reinforce those new pathways.

This is the internal work of mastering the heart of the sale.

You're not just trying to "think more positively." You're choosing a new story. One where sales is not about convincing, it's about connecting. Where serving isn't a tactic, it's the foundation.

And every time you do, you're not just changing your mind.

You're transforming your life, and everyone you're here to serve. Before you lead a team, a business, or even a sales call, you must first lead yourself. Sales, at its core, is not about the hustle, the perfect pitch, or the clever close. It's about **alignment, empathy,** and **clarity of purpose.** It's about **selling from the heart.**

We've all seen it, the one-tonality pitch, the robotic script, the desperate rush to convince someone into a "yes." That's not sales. That's noise. That's fear talking. And it's what 99% of people fall into when they don't know better. But you do. Or at least, you're about to. I often say — *"I leave that kind of selling to the 'salespeople'… in quotes."* The ones who think sales is about pushing product rather than offering value. You're not here to sell in that way. You're here to serve.

Here's your new mindset:

"I'm not here to sell. I'm here to understand."

That means asking great questions. It means getting under the hood, really seeing the person in front of you, not just as a prospect, but as a human being with desires, hesitations, fears, and goals. Your job is to connect their needs with your solution, *but only if it genuinely aligns.*

When you approach sales this way, it becomes something else entirely. It becomes a powerful conversation. An honest connection. A moment where both people walk away feeling aligned, congruent, and grateful for the time spent.

So how do you show up to those conversations?

Not physically, mentally. Energetically. Emotionally.

Are you aligned with what you're selling?

Do you believe in it? Live it? Embody it?

Because if you're asking someone to say yes to something you wouldn't say yes to yourself, there's a disconnect, and they'll feel it. People can spot misalignment a mile away. But when you're in it, when your product or service is an extension of your values, your growth, and your truth, that's when magic happens.

Here's a real golden nugget I want to drop in right here, because it's one of those mindsets shifts that once you hear it, you can't unhear it.

Whether you believe in God, the Big Bang, or any origin story in between, there's one universal truth we can all agree on:

When the Earth was formed, it was made with gold and silver.

Think about that for a second.

Gold and silver have always been part of this planet. They're not man-made inventions. They weren't created by economies or entrepreneurs. They were already here woven into the fabric of Earth itself.
Now take that in from a human and business perspective.

You are from the Earth.

You were formed from the same elements.

You carry that gold and silver *within you.*

What does that mean?

It means that value, exchange, and trade are part of your natural DNA. From the very beginning, long before business plans and branding, there was bartering. Gold for silver. Goats for beans. Services for shelter. *We were designed to trade, to exchange, to serve, to sell.*

Let that sink in:

Selling isn't unnatural. It's not slimy. It's sacred.

It's the hard-sell, pushy, manipulative tactics that feel off, not the act of selling itself.

You're not wrong for wanting to make an offer.
You're not pushy for wanting to be paid.
You're not salesy for valuing what you bring to the table.
You're just remembering something ancient.

We were always supposed to do this.

Sales is simply a form of connection and contribution.
It's in our bones.

When you embrace that truth, when you drop the old story that sales is something to avoid or be ashamed of, you open the door to doing it differently. Authentically. Congruently. In alignment with who you are. And that's what this book is about.

It's not just about strategies and scripts, though we'll absolutely cover those. It's about the heart behind it. The energy within it. The soul of sales. Because a sale, at its highest level, is a relationship. A sacred exchange. So, here's your permission slip:

You were made for this.

And now, we're going to do it the right way.

Self-Leadership is The Foundation of Authentic Sales
Let's get real: You cannot lead others, inspire trust, or create loyal clients if you're not managing your own inner game. You must be crystal clear on:

Who you want to be.
What's stopping you from being that.
And how to start showing up as that person, right now.

Let's pause.

If I could wave a magic wand and you could step into your ultimate future self, what does that look like?

Where do you live?
What holidays are planned?
What kind of car are you driving?
How do you spend your time?
What service or product are you offering to the world?

And most importantly, how aligned are you with your values and the thing you're inviting others to invest in?

Write it down.

There's power in writing. Frequency. Energy. Momentum.

Because here's the truth: If you can define where you want to be, I want to know why you're not there yet.

What's really holding you back?

Write these things down, too. No filters.

Are you too young?
Too old?
Not qualified enough.
Does imposter syndrome creep in?
Is someone in your life telling you it's silly?
Do you tell yourself you don't have enough time, confidence, or clarity?

Whatever the story, bring it to the surface. Because awareness is the beginning of breakthrough.

Reframing the Fluff: Become Conscious of Your Patterns

Let me share something with you. Have you noticed how people always talk about the weather?

"It's too hot."
"It's too cold."
"It's always raining."

We laugh and say, *"Oh, it's just an English thing."* But it's not. It's a **global habit.** It's fluff. It's learned behaviour. We repeat patterns without even realising it.

Here's a simple reframe you can use:

Next time someone comments on the weather, stop them in their tracks.

Say, "Isn't it an incredible system? The sun, the rain, the snow... the seasons, it's brilliant. I love how nature just works."

Watch their face.
You've just **broken the pattern.**
You've made them **think.**

That's how it starts. That's how transformation begins.
You break the unconscious loop and choose a new response.

Manage Yourself. Align Yourself. Become the Product.

Now let's bring it back to you. If you're trying to sell something you're not living, you're out of sync. Full stop.

There's this idea floating around that great salespeople don't need to know their product inside out. Total nonsense.

You must know it. Live it. Feel it. Use it. Love it. You must be it.

I've worked with countless businesses, from innovation to retail, service-based businesses to training providers, and the one constant in every success story is this: alignment and ownership.

When I worked with a window company, I implemented my training systems and mindset strategies. Each time I came in, sales would spike. Morale would soar. People would connect. But after two weeks, they'd fall back. Back to hustle. Back to misalignment. Because the leadership didn't care about the client experience or their people, they only cared about the numbers.

I realised - I wasn't aligned. And I walked away.

Because when you lead from the heart, when you truly serve, the right people will feel it. And the money? It becomes a byproduct of value. A result of resonance.

So, here's your challenge:

Lead yourself.
Before you lead anyone else.

Write your vision.
Where are you headed?

Live your product
Become the walking embodiment of what you sell.

Reframe the fluff
Become conscious of your patterns.

List your blocks
What's holding you back?

This is how you lead your mind.
This is how you lead your business.
This is how you sell from the heart.

System and Routines: Structure That Sets You Free

If mindset is the engine of a service-driven entrepreneur, then systems and routines is the oil that keeps it running smoothly. You can have all the heart, all the empathy, and all the passion in the world, but without structure, your brilliance will burn out fast.

Here's the truth: Service doesn't mean chaos. In fact, genuine service thrives in systems. Why? Because when your calendar is in order, your client journey is mapped, your follow-ups are automatic, and your operations are clear, *you're free to show up fully*. You're not drowning in the "what next?" or scrambling for missing pieces. You're present. You're effective. And you're consistent.

Routines aren't just for productivity; they are a form of respect. Respect for your mission. Respect for your clients. Respect for yourself.

Creating a system might look like:
- A morning routine that primes your mind for purpose, not panic.
- A CRM that keeps every client nurtured and never forgotten.
- A checklist for every discovery call that ensures no need goes unnoticed.
- A weekly time block to review, reflect, and refine.

And let's be clear: this doesn't mean becoming robotic. This is conscious automation. You build frameworks so you can focus on what only you can do, serve from the heart. Selling with soul requires repeatability. Systems give you that. Routines protect your energy, your creativity, and your ability to keep showing up for the people you're called to serve.

Let me ask you something.

Have you ever had a stretch in life where everything just clicks? You're on it - eating clean, exercising, not constantly drinking alcohol, showing up sharp, focused, energised. You're in your zone. Business is better. Your relationships feel smoother. Your confidence rises. Life flows.
Then, suddenly... you fall off.

Not catastrophically. Just subtly at first. One drink becomes a few. You skip the gym once, then twice. You slip back into default habits - the ones you picked up as a kid or learned from your peers growing up. The energy shifts. Business slows. Frustration creeps in. And you find yourself back in that cycle - up and down like a rollercoaster at Alton Towers.

Sound familiar?

That was my reality. I didn't realise it at the time, but I was caught in a loop - a system of dysfunction disguised as normality. My routines weren't intentional. They were inherited, reactionary, emotional defaults.

At 39, everything came crashing down. Divorce. Business burnout. A brain tumour diagnosis. And worst of all, I had fallen out of love with myself. I'd look in the mirror and feel nothing but disconnection. I didn't recognise the man staring back at me - and worse, I didn't like him. There was no fire in his eyes. No conviction. Just survival. And the thought that haunted me was:

"This isn't who I was meant to be."

I drove to the pub that day to drown my sorrows - again. I lifted the pint to my lips, and in that moment, I caught a glimpse of someone at the other end of the bar. A local bloke I'd known years ago. Twenty years older. Lovely guy. Charismatic. But as I looked at him, I saw my future. A version of me - still telling stories, still at the pub, still stuck.

I put the pint down, walked out, got in the car, and drove. And cried. And drove. And cried some more.

And I asked myself:

How did I end up here?
How do I become the man I know I was created to be?

That moment changed everything.

For the first time in my life, I stopped searching outward for the fix - whether it was food, drink, distraction or validation and I looked inward. Not for answers, but for alignment. I began studying the greats. From Tony Robbins to Henry Ford, from elite athletes to world-class entrepreneurs. What made them different?

They were intentional.

They didn't leave their lives to chance. They had systems. They had routines. They showed up on purpose. Daily.

Here's what I discovered:
Everything you need to become your best self is free.

That's right - free.

You don't need to buy a magic pill or an expensive program. You were born with the tools. You just need to use them.

The Four Foundational Routines That Changed My Life:

Breathwork
Ten deep, conscious breaths. Inhale, hold, exhale. It grounds you. It centres you. It reconnects you to the present.

Mindfulness & Visualisation
Take five quiet minutes in the morning and at night. Visualise the person you want to become. Feel that version of you. Don't just think it - embody it.

Movement
Whether it's a walk around the block, yoga, or dancing in the kitchen - move your body. Energy needs motion to flow. If you're breathing, you can move.

Cold Water Therapy
Even a 30-second cold shower at the end of your hot one builds discipline, shocks your system, and wakes up your soul.

These routines aren't just hacks—they're anchors. They are the scaffolding that supports your mindset, your energy, and your results. You don't need to do all of them at once. Start with one. Just one. And do it daily. Stack it with intention. Then, after 7 days, add another. Keep going. 21 days. 90 days. Let it compound. This isn't about perfection—it's about momentum.

"Be intentional about being intentional."

That's not just a catchy phrase. That's the key to building a sustainable life and business. When you start your day with purpose, you show up to your sales calls different. You speak with clarity. You listen with depth. You don't fake energy - you are energy.

Your clients will feel it. Your family will feel it. You'll feel it.

And here's the wildest thing...

People will start asking, "What's changed about you?" And you'll smile because you'll know: you stopped reacting to life and started designing it.

So let me land this chapter with something simple:

The 1% Rule
Each week, add one thing that serves you.
And take away one thing that doesn't.

Do this for 90 days. That's 12 new positive habits. 12 harmful ones gone. That's not minor - that's transformational.

You don't need to overhaul your life overnight. Just start today. One percent at a time.

Because here's the truth:

"If you don't create your system, the world will give you one, and it won't serve you."

So, build the version of you that you want to wake up to.

You deserve to look in the mirror and love what you see, not just the face, but the fire behind the eyes. That's the reward of routines. That's the power of systems.

That's the secret to living, loving, and leading... on purpose.

When your internal world (mindset) and external world (systems) align, that's when selling becomes a flow, not a fight.

Inspire and Rewire: Shifting Thought Patterns to Serve Powerfully

To truly embrace a service-oriented mindset, you need more than motivation, you need transformation. That's where the power of inspiration and rewiring comes in.

Inspiration is the spark. It's the moment something in your spirit says, "This is possible." But rewiring, that's the real shift. That's where you retrain your brain to respond, act, and lead in a new way. Because if your default thought patterns are rooted in fear, scarcity, or self-doubt, no amount of surface-level inspiration will sustain you.

Here's what we need to get honest about: Most of us have internal programming around sales that's outdated, inherited, or simply unhelpful. Maybe we were taught that selling means pushing - That asking equals begging - That money is dirty, or service means sacrifice. You can't serve powerfully if you secretly believe sales is wrong.

Rewiring starts with awareness. You begin to notice your inner narrative:

- Do I feel guilty about charging?
- Do I shrink when it's time to make the offer?
- Do I assume people will say no before I even ask?

Once you notice, you can challenge those beliefs and replace them. This isn't fluff. Neuroscience backs it. When you repeatedly think a thought, your brain forms a neural pathway. The more you walk that path, the stronger it gets. Rewiring simply means walking a new path – again and again – until it becomes your new normal.

You inspire yourself daily by consuming what lifts you, surrounding yourself with people who believe in service-based selling, and choosing thoughts that empower rather than limit. Then you rewire by taking aligned action.

You say the new thought.
You show up with the new energy.
You close the sale with integrity.
You serve without apologising.

That's how we build a new sales identity, one that's heart-centred, rooted in service, and anchored in belief. Because before you can help someone else transform, you must believe in the value of what you offer. And that begins in the mind.

So now that you've started to Inspire and Rewire, let's go deeper.
It's time to zoom in on you – not just the 'you' that shows up for others, but the version of you that you see in your mind's eye. The one you could be, the one you want to be, the one you were perhaps closer to as a child, before life started layering expectations and limitations on top.

Let's start with this:

- Who inspires you?
- Who are your role models?

They could be public figures, people in your industry, a mentor, a close friend, even a family member. Someone whose story stirs something deep within you. Someone whose qualities make you want to grow. Someone who, simply by being themselves, reminds you that you can be more of yourself too.

Make a list.

Not just names - dig into why.

* What is it about them that lights something up in you?
* What values do they seem to embody?
* What beliefs do they hold?
* What are they committed to?
* What does their energy feel like?
Are they confident? Grounded? Brave? Soft? Kind?
What have they achieved that resonates with you?
What's their story? And how do you relate to it?
This isn't about comparison - it's about connection.

You're not meant to be them. You're meant to become you - but perhaps a truer, bolder, more authentic version. And looking at those who inspire you is one of the fastest ways to reconnect to what's already inside you.

The Truth About Who You Are.

People ask me how I've become the version of myself I am today, how I went from being in a wheelchair after a brain tumour to now feeling more mentally, emotionally, and physically alive than I ever did before Here's what I tell them:

"I didn't change who I was. I just got out of my own way."

I stripped back the layers of ego, doubt, fear, perfectionism, and old pain. And underneath it all - I found me. The real me. The version I've been all along. The version I knew as a kid.

Remember that child you once were? Before life happened. Before the doubts came.

What did you dream about? Who did you want to become?
That child is still in you.

The closer we get back to that pure version of ourselves, the closer we get to the truth. That's what this journey is about - coming home to yourself.

Stop Using Your Past as Proof

You might be telling yourself that you've failed before, so why would this time be different?

Let me reframe that: There are no failures - only learnings.

Everything you've been through has taught you something. If a business didn't work, you learnt something. If a relationship ended, you learnt something. If you invested in yourself ten times before and didn't see the result, guess what? That's not failure. That's training.

So, stop lining up your past and using it as proof that your future will be the same.

Your past is not your potential.

You have the power, right now, to choose a new story.

Visualise the Future.

Now think about your future self.

The one you'd admire. The one who's living with intention.

That version of you, confident, successful, fulfilled, joyful.

Visualise it in detail. Picture your business, your lifestyle, your relationships, your energy. Picture it all – and then decide:

Who do I need to become to live that life?

Because the truth is: you can.

You can be the person you admire.

You can live that life.

You can feel that way.

But you must be intentional, be Intentional About Being Intentional Here's a line I want you to remember:

I am so intentional about being intentional, I don't leave my growth to chance.

I don't hope for change – I create it.

And that takes systems. It takes habits. It takes deliberate choices repeated daily until they become who you are. You don't "become" overnight. You evolve. You show up day after day and you build the version of yourself you want to be.

Let me share a simple practice that's helped me – and thousands of others – rewire their mind, reclaim their power, and become more present.

1. Morning Gratitude - Before the world grabs you, before the phone, emails, notifications, pause.
2. Write down 3 things you're truly grateful for - something real. Something felt. Something that brings you back to the moment.

It could be:
* That you're alive.
* That you can walk, breathe, think.
* That you have people who love you.
* That you've got another shot today.

Start there. Gratitude shifts your mindset. It roots you in abundance.

Daily Intentions

Write down 3 things you want to achieve today.

Not a giant to-do list - just 3 things that move you closer to the person you're becoming.

Maybe it's making a sales call, writing content, working out, connecting with someone meaningfully. Be deliberate. Choose progress over perfection.

Evening Reflection

At the end of the day, switch off your phone. Create space.
Reflect:

* Did I show up the way I wanted to today?
* What did I learn?
* What am I proud of?
* What's one good thing I did for someone else?

Could be a kind message. Picking up litter. Saying sorry. Reaching out. Smiling at a stranger. Impact doesn't have to be big to be meaningful.

Mindfulness & Meditation

These tiny habits, gratitude, intent, reflection, they're all part of something bigger: becoming mindful. When you become more conscious of how you think, speak, move, and feel, your entire life shifts. You begin to own your days instead of reacting to them. If you can add just a few minutes of stillness, through meditation, breathing, or silence, you'll start noticing how much clearer, calmer, and more in control you feel.

Even 2 minutes. That's enough to begin.

And the best part? All of this is free.

Joy is free.

Peace is free.

Love is free.

Becoming your best self? That's a choice.

Final Thoughts for This Chapter

You are not broken. You are becoming.

You're not here to hustle for your worth, you're here to remember it.

So, write your list.

Identify your role models.

Reflect on who you admire, and why.

Recognise that those very traits already live inside of you.

Now start building the bridge between where you are and who you want to be.

Not with pressure.

Not with force.

But with consistent, intentional action.

Because when you align your thoughts, your values, and your actions with your vision...

You don't just dream about the life you want - you start living.

Navigate the Hurdles & Be the Best Version of You

Up to this point, we've explored how to reset your mindset, take daily intentional action, and rewire yourself for growth. But now, let's get real. Because no matter how much inner work you do, challenge will show up. Life isn't predictable. One day might feel like a breakthrough, and the next, like you're right back where you started.

So, let's talk about how to navigate the hurdles and still show up as the best version of you.

Here's the truth: even when you're doing the work, life will test you. You might feel triggered by something that reminds you of a past failure. You may think, "I've invested in myself so many times before and never seen the return, why would this time be any different?

But here's the catch: if you're already in that mindset, how can you help someone else shift theirs?

If a potential client is stuck in a story about why things won't work, and deep down, YOU believe that story too, you're going to subconsciously agree with them. That's sympathy. And sympathy in a sales conversation? It's a silent killer. Because when you sympathise, you step into their limitations with them instead of leading them out.

Empathy connects. Sympathy keeps you stuck.

So, let's do the work now to unpick the stories that have been keeping you stuck.

Think back:

* What investments have you made in the past that didn't work out?
* Were you all in? Did you fully commit?
* Or did you do the surface work and hope for deep results?

Be honest with yourself.

Maybe it was a diet, a course, a new habit, or a big business leap. Maybe you didn't get the result you wanted. That's okay. But what did you tell yourself after that?

Most people stay trapped in a loop:

"It didn't work before… so it won't work now."

That thinking stops everything. It's the reason people stay stuck.

So, if that's where you've been living, how can you expect someone to buy into your offer, your coaching, your product - when you haven't even bought into yourself?

Let's flip it. What story do you need to start telling yourself instead?

Because here's what I know: transformation takes commitment. It takes consistent, intentional action. You can't just dip a toe in' and expect to swim across an ocean.

This is your 7-day, 21-day, 30-day, 60-day, or 90-day commitment to change your world. But it only works if you 'go all in'.

Let's look at an example. I often ask audiences this when I'm speaking:

What's a large amount of money to you?

Write it down.

What's a small amount of money to you?

Write that down too.

Here's why this matters – because your perception of money directly affects your ability to sell. If your idea of a 'large amount' is £1,000, and your product is priced at £2,000... then you'll subconsciously believe your own product is too expensive.

So, when someone says, "That's a lot of money," you'll agree with them, and you'll lose the sale.

But what if your mindset was:

"This offer is powerful. It creates real transformation. £2,000 is an investment – not a cost."

That energy shift matters. Because when you stand in belief, your client can too.

Let's get practical:

- What thinking loops are holding you back?
- Where have you self-sabotaged by playing small or giving up early?
- Where are you afraid to go all in, because of past disappointments?

Identify them. Write them down. Own them.

Then ask:

- Did I fully commit?
- Did I follow the plan?
- Or did I just hope things would change without truly changing?

Once you're clear, decide:
- what needs to shift? What new story do you need to believe?

Because the version of you that gets results? That version shows up differently. That version is present, intentional, and open.

Fear Has Many Faces. Name Yours.

What fear is holding you back?
- Fear of failure?
- Fear of success?
- Fear of change?
- Fear of being seen?
- Fear that this might actually work?

You're not alone. We all carry these at some point. But if you let fear dictate your actions, you'll never experience what you're truly capable of.

The good news?

Fear can't survive in the present moment. If you're truly present - right here, right now - fear fades. Anxiety fades. All that's left is connection.

So go into every sales conversation, every opportunity, every relationship... with presence. Be there. Ask better questions. Listen more. Connect deeply.

Don't chase a sale. **Open a relationship.**

And if it's not the right fit? That's okay. Serve them by pointing them to someone who is the right fit. That's leadership. That's service.
Final Thought on this - Enjoy the Process

You're building something meaningful. You're creating a new version of yourself. So, enjoy it. Be present in the moments between the milestones. Celebrate the progress. Laugh. Connect. Keep showing up.

Because the real win isn't in the sale.

It's in becoming the version of you who doesn't need to sell to win - because you're already living and breathing the value you offer.

Build the business and the dream

Develop and Dream

You can't scale what you haven't defined. So, before we talk about systems, monetisation, or next-level strategies, we need to get painfully, radically clear on this: What is it that you do? What do you sell? How much is it?

Right now, if I asked you that question, could you give me a clear, concise, confident answer? No fluff. No five-minute backstory. Just straight truth. Because if you can't answer that, you've got work to do.

The truth is, one of the biggest mistakes I see entrepreneurs make -especially heart-led coaches, creatives, and service providers - is failing to define what they offer in a way that lands with their audience. They know their craft inside out. They're deeply passionate. But they're fuzzy in their delivery. That confusion creates friction. And confused people do not buy.

So, let's clean it up. Get super specific. Not just about what you love to do - but what your audience wants. What is the demand for your offer? What's trending in your market? What language does your dream client use when they talk about the problem you solve? You don't even have to guess. Use tools like ChatGPT or keyword searches to test and shape your messaging. Let the data help you - but make sure your final version still sounds like you. Tweak it. Humanise it. Sharpen it until it cuts through the noise.

Now, here's a key exercise I recommend for every entrepreneur at every stage:

Build your client avatar.

Create a detailed profile of your ideal customer. Give them a name, an age, a career, a lifestyle. What are they struggling with? What are they dreaming about? What keeps them awake at night? What have they tried before that didn't work? And, most importantly, what would make them say "finally!" when they hear about your offer?

This isn't fluff. This is the difference between launching into a cold, disconnected sales pitch versus stepping into a warm, aligned, soul-led conversation. Because when you deeply understand who you serve, your offer becomes a gift, not a gamble.

Let's go deeper.

Write this down right now:

What is the #1 pain point you solve?

- What is the thing your service, product, or program helps them overcome?

- What has your own experience taught you that now allows you to guide others through it?

Now flip it.

What is the result they get from working with you?

What are the specific outcomes? The transformation? What's they're "after" story? How does your process deliver that, clearly and effectively?

The goal here is clarity, not complexity. One of the reasons so many entrepreneurs struggle to sell is because they overexplain. They go too deep, too soon, trying to prove the value through volume. And what happens? They either confuse their prospect, or worse, push them back into hesitation.

Let me remind you of something powerful:

People don't like to be sold to. But they love to buy.

So the art is in inviting, not impressing. Guiding, not overwhelming. If you can clearly state what you do, who you do it for, the problem you solve, the results you help them achieve, and how much it costs, you will instantly stand out in a sea of noise. Say it like you're speaking to a 10-year-old. Not because your clients aren't intelligent, but because clarity creates confidence, and confidence converts.
Here's an example:

"I help business owners sell without feeling like a sleazy salesperson by using a simple, heart-based method.

I deliver it through a 3-day program called 'The Heart of the Sale,' which covers six transformational pillars.

The price is X. That leads into my longer-term academy, which is Y."
Clear. Confident. Direct. No fluff, no dance.

Be proud of your price. Don't bury it in the small print. Say it early. Say it with certainty. Let the value speak for itself.

If your audience is constantly confused, asking too many questions, or walking away to "think about it", chances are, you're either unclear or overwhelming. Either way, you've lost them.

So today, your homework is this:

- Create your customer avatar (using the worksheet below)
- Define the pain point you solve.
- Clarify the outcome you deliver.
- Write your one-sentence pitch: "I help X do Y without Z, through this method."
- Be able to confidently explain your delivery method, your offer, and your pricing.
- Practice saying it out loud until it feels natural, not rehearsed.

Because the dream can only be built on what is defined. And once you develop that clarity, that focus, that aligned offer - your dream isn't just something you imagine. It's something you build.

Client Avatar Clarity (Designer to create Worksheet)

Name Your Avatar:

(Give them a name so they feel real. Example: "Confused Cathy" or "Determined Danielle")

Demographics
- Age:
- Gender:
- Location:
- Job Title/Career:
- Income Range:
- Education Level:
- Relationship/Family Status:

Psychographics

- Core Values:
- Biggest Dreams:
- Biggest Fears:
- What keeps them up at night?
- What motivates them to take action?

Pain Points

- What are their top 3 frustrations?
- What problems are they actively trying to solve?
- What have they tried before that didn't work?
- What limiting beliefs might be holding them back?

Desired Outcomes

- What transformation do they want most?
- What does "success" look like to them?
- How would their life or business be different if this problem was solved?

Communication Clues

- What language or phrases do they use to describe their problem?
- What words or tone would resonate with them?
- What platforms do they hang out on? (Instagram, LinkedIn, Facebook, etc.)

Your Offer Match

- How does your product or service directly address their pain points?
- What result does your solution create for them?
- What's the delivery method (coaching, course, product, service, event)?
- How will you price it and explain it clearly?

Now that we've unpacked the need to build by knowing your ideal client, the hurdles, thought loops, the fear patterns, the old narratives, let's shift our energy. Let's move into the space where transformation truly takes root: developing yourself into the person you're meant to be and giving yourself full permission to dream again.

Because here's the truth: once you've identified what's held you back, you've got a choice to make. You can stay there - looping, blaming, hesitating, or you can build. And building starts from the inside out. It's time to develop new standards, new patterns, and a new belief system that supports the version of you you're growing into. You want to be exceptional in business? You want to sell with heart and soul? Then you've got to develop a mindset and a rhythm that supports that. No more operating from a place of fear, lack, or "just enough." This part of the journey is about designing your days, training your focus, and elevating your inner environment so that your outer world starts to shift.

This is develop and dream. It's about raising your standards, not just in what you expect from others, but what you demand from yourself. Because if you don't raise your own standards, the world won't either.

But development without a dream is just motion without meaning. So, let's get bold.

What is the dream?

What are you building? What vision excites you, scares you, challenges you, and wakes you up in the middle of the night?

Write it down. Don't overthink it. Don't edit it. Don't censor it based on what you think you're "allowed" to want. Dream from the part of you that knows you were meant for more. Because that part of you - that truth - it's not random. It's the invitation.

You were given the dream because you're the one who can bring it to life.

But dreams need roots. They need structure. They need daily action and radical commitment. That's the development piece. That's the work behind the scenes. That's the early mornings, the quiet hours, the inner battles you win when nobody's watching. That's where your edge is built.

And here's the beautiful thing: the bigger your dream, the deeper your development. They rise together. As you develop, your dream expands. As your dream grows, it calls a greater version of you forward. That's the dance.

So, this chapter, this moment, is about answering two questions:

1. Who do I want to become?
2. What am I here to create?

Your dream is the map.

Your daily development is the vehicle.

And your decision to go all in, every single day, is the fuel.

Don't just want it. **Walk it.**

Don't just dream it. **Develop it.**

Because when you become the person who doesn't quit, who doesn't self-sabotage, who doesn't shrink back, that's when the world starts to notice. That's when clients feel your certainty. That's when people lean in and say, "I don't know what it is about you, but I trust you."

That's when authentic sales become effortless. Because people aren't just buying your product - they're buying into your energy, your clarity, your belief.

You want to stand out in a noisy marketplace?

Develop yourself. Dream bigger. And then go again.

Systems and Routines

Now let us take a quick look at systems and routines, I believe it's Jim Rohn that once said, *"Discipline is the bridge between goals and accomplishment." – Jim Rohn*

As we move from skill into structure, it's time to shift gears, from dreaming to doing. Many entrepreneurs spend their energy constantly chasing the next big idea or client, but without a repeatable process, burnout is inevitable. The truth is: your success isn't built on how many hours you work; it's built on how well your systems work for you.

Heart-centred entrepreneurs often resist structure, thinking it will stifle their flow or authenticity. But in reality, systems and routines are what set you free to serve more, stress less, and sell with soul. They don't restrict your creativity, they protect it.

When you put systems in place that reflect your values, you create a business that not only runs smoothly but also resonates deeply with those you serve.

Many entrepreneurs dream big but get stuck in the doing, spinning in busy-ness without consistent progress. The difference between those who dabble and those who thrive.

Systems
Routines
Rituals

These are not restrictions, they are your liberation.
They give your brilliance a channel.
They make your magic repeatable.

They free up your mental space so you can serve, sell, and scale with more clarity and less stress.

Why does systems matter, especially in heart-centred Sales?

A lot of heart-led entrepreneurs resist structure. You might fear it'll box you in or make your business feel mechanical. But the opposite is true:

- Systems support your flow.
- Routines protect your energy.
- Structure allows for spontaneity, without the burnout.

Selling from the heart still requires a strategy. Love alone won't create consistent income. You need a system that allows your values to breathe through every step of your business, from lead generation to sales calls to client onboarding.

Build Rhythm, Not Rigidity

Here's the truth: You don't need a complex system; you need a repeatable rhythm.

Start by anchoring your week with high-impact routines:

Weekly CEO Rituals
- Reflect on wins and lessons
- Review key metrics (leads, calls booked, income, impact)
- Plan intentional actions: What will move the needle this week?

Daily Anchors
- Morning mindset and intention-setting
- Power Hour (1 focused hour for income-producing activities)
- Client love and outreach
- Evening review: What worked? What needs tweaking?

Heart-centred selling becomes sustainable when it's supported by systems such as:

- A **lead tracker** that tells you who to follow up with and when
- A **content calendar** aligned with your offers and launches
- A **sales script or framework** that keeps you grounded in service, not pressure
- A **CRM or spreadsheet** that reminds you of key dates, touchpoints, and opportunities
- A **calendar strategy** that includes space for creation, calls, and rest

Even the most soulful sales process thrives with a backbone.

For example:

Let's say you offer 1:1 coaching. A simple weekly routine might look like:
- **Monday:** Set intentions, review leads, send 5 connection DMs
- **Tuesday:** Content creation, follow-ups
- **Wednesday:** Discovery calls
- **Thursday:** Client sessions
- **Friday:** Admin, testimonials, CEO review

This isn't rigid, it's rhythmic. You can still flow, but now with purpose.

Your dream deserves a container. Your clients deserve consistency. And you deserve to feel like the leader of your business, not its exhausted employee.

Systems give your heart a megaphone.
Routines give your mission legs.
Structure gives your genius a home.

Creating routines isn't just about what you get done. It's about who you're becoming. When you commit to routines that honour your goals and your boundaries, you begin to embody the version of you who leads with clarity, confidence, and calm.

And when your clients see that?
- They trust you more.
- They invest more.
- Everybody wins.

REMEMBER – YOU ARE THE STRATEGY

By now, you've seen that success in sales doesn't start with scripts or closing tactics. It starts with you. Your mindset, your skills, your dreams, your systems, these are the roots that allow your business to grow with authenticity and purpose.

When you ground yourself in service and structure, you're no longer chasing sales, you're creating space for aligned clients to find you, trust you, and say yes with confidence. You're not just learning how to sell, you're learning how to show up: for yourself, for your mission, and for those you're here to serve.

This chapter isn't about checking boxes, it's about building a foundation that reflects the kind of business and legacy you're here to create. One where strategy meets soul. Where clarity leads to confidence. Where structure creates freedom.

As you move into the next chapter, keep this truth close:

You don't need to become someone else to succeed in sales. You just need to become more of who you really are - aligned, prepared, and committed to serving.

Let's move forward and explore how to create a sales strategy that feels like service, not persuasion. Because when it's built from the heart, everybody wins.

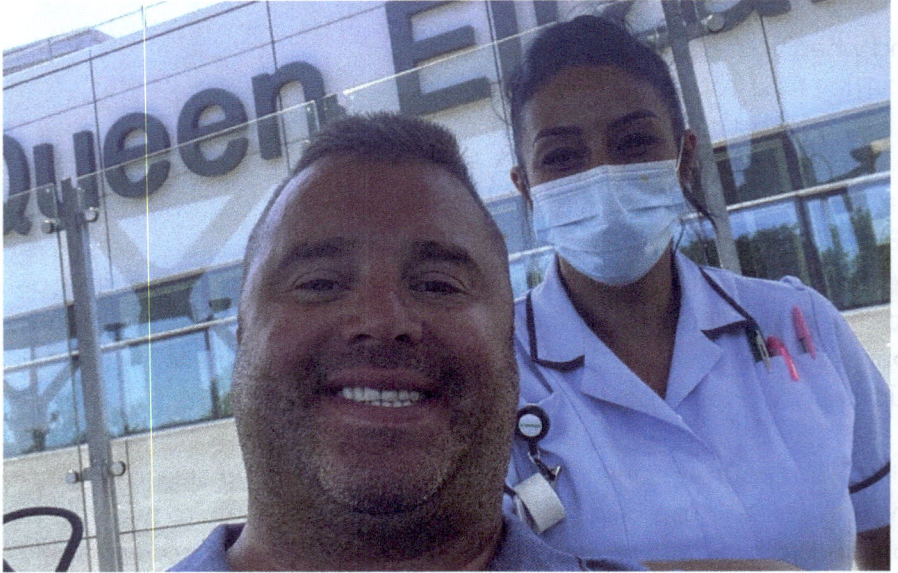

After my Operation

BRAIN TUMOUR RESEARCH
NATIONAL 3 PEAKS CHALLENGE

DONATE NOW TO SUPPORT
BRAIN TUMOUR RESEARCH

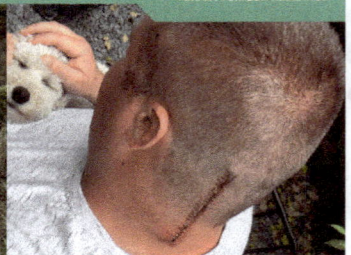

HELP MARCUS AND 5 FRIENDS
RAISE MONEY FOR A CHARITY
CLOSE TO THEIR HEARTS

Fundraising for
Brain Tumour
Research

Raising funds for Brain Tumour Research

marcus elwell

SALES MINDSET TRANSFORMATION

CHAPTER THREE

SERVICE

Elevating Your Skills And Impact

At its core, selling is an act of service. It's not about pushing a product or closing a deal, it's about deeply understanding someone's needs and helping them move closer to the life or solution they truly desire. When done with intention, service-based selling becomes a powerful bridge between your gift and the transformation your client is seeking.

In this chapter, we step beyond the basics of connection and mindset and into the mechanics of mastery. You'll learn how to fine-tune your approach, communicate with greater clarity, and remove any lingering internal resistance that keeps you from fully showing up in your power. It's here that your skills are sharpened, not through manipulation, but through alignment with your values and the results you know you can deliver. True service requires presence. It requires the willingness to observe, to listen deeper than words, and to respond in a way that empowers the person in front of you. It calls for confidence, rooted not in perfection, but in preparation and purpose. As we move forward, you'll begin to see sales not as a performance, but as a co-created experience. One where transformation is not just promised, but embodied, from the very first conversation. When you serve with intention, with empathy, and with skill, everybody wins.

Service is where skill meets sincerity.

If mindset is the foundation and clarity is your compass, service is your movement, your forward momentum. It's the act of showing up, not to pitch, but to truly serve. And the more skilled you are at delivering that service clearly, confidently, and with heart, the more magnetic and impactful your presence becomes.

So, let me ask you: are you ready to level up your ability to serve with excellence?

Let's start with a moment of honesty. Most people don't have a sales problem, they have a clarity and communication problem. When you can't articulate your value clearly, concisely, and confidently, you unconsciously invite confusion or hesitation from the people you're meant to help.

This chapter is about eliminating that confusion.

It's about making sure that what you offer lands so cleanly, so powerfully, that the right people can't help but say yes.

And that begins with becoming a student of service. Great salespeople, heart-centred, high-converting, integrity-driven salespeople, aren't just winging it. They're deliberate. They study people. They listen more than they speak. They refine their approach constantly. They understand buyer psychology. They embrace objections instead of resisting them. And most importantly, they serve without attachment to the outcome. That's where your next level lives.

We're going to dive into what I call your Service Intelligence, a combination of strategy, skill, empathy, and structure. This is where you start to unlock conversations that flow, offers that convert, and relationships that last well beyond the transaction. It's time to stop seeing sales as a standalone skill and start understanding it as the natural extension of service. When done right, your offer becomes the vehicle of someone else's transformation.

In this chapter, we'll explore the shifts you need to make, from chasing to attracting, from guessing to guiding, from selling to serving. You'll learn how to:

- Understand your buyer better than they understand themselves.
- Identify and break through belief blocks, both yours and theirs.
- Handle objections with heart and confidence.
- Anchor your message in meaningful outcomes, not just features or price.
- Deliver your value so clearly that people feel empowered to say yes.

Because when you lead with service, everybody wins.

Let's begin.

Buyers Strategy

Sales is less about pushing a product and more about deeply understanding who you're speaking to. The key to successful sales lies in the ability to tailor your communication to the psychology of your buyer. This chapter dives into the art and science of identifying different buyer types and how you can adjust your approach to serve each one more effectively. Sales isn't about convincing someone to buy, it's about understanding why they buy and how they decide. The most effective salespeople don't rely on rehearsed scripts; they rely on emotional intelligence and buyer psychology. This chapter equips you to identify your prospect's buying style and shift your approach accordingly.

You've probably heard the phrase: "People buy with emotion and justify with logic." That's true for most buyers, but it doesn't mean everyone buys for the same reasons or in the same way.

Think of it this way: just as people have different learning styles, visual, auditory, kinaesthetic, they also have different buying styles. Your job is to become a student of human behaviour. The better you understand what drives someone to buy, the easier it becomes to guide them toward the solution you offer.

To connect deeply and serve authentically, you must learn to speak your buyer's language. That begins with identifying their decision-making style.

Let's look at the four core buyer types, how to recognise them, and how to adjust your sales strategy to better support them.

1. The Dominant Buyer: The Decisive Driver

This buyer is confident, assertive, and results oriented. They want the bottom line, and they want it fast. Dominant buyers are often leaders, executives, entrepreneurs, people who make decisions quickly and don't need to be hand-held through the process.

How to Spot Them:

- They get straight to the point
- They're confident, sometimes blunt
- They often interrupt or redirect the conversation
- They make quick decisions and dislike small talk

Buyer Strategy:

Lead with value.
Start the conversation with what they'll gain.

Position your offer as a power move
Show how it advances their mission or elevates their status.

Be efficient
Present the outcome, not a lengthy backstory.

Use assertive language
"Here's what I recommend," "Let's move forward," "This is the winning strategy."

Tip: Dominant buyers respond well to strong leadership. Match their intensity while maintaining calm authority, as they appreciate confidence and decisiveness. If you waffle or over-explain, you'll lose them. Think of this buyer as someone who would respond to: *"Here's what I can do, here's how it will help you win, and here's the next step."*

2. The Analytical Buyer: The Thoughtful Researcher

Analytical buyers are all about the details. They want data, proof, comparisons, and logic. These buyers are methodical and cautious, they don't make quick decisions, but once they do, they rarely backtrack.

Key Traits: Logical, precise, cautious, process-driven
Primary Question: "Is this the smartest and most reliable choice?"

These buyers live in spreadsheets and want everything to make sense before they take action. Their decisions are based on facts, not feelings.

How to Spot Them:
- They ask many clarifying questions
- They rarely show strong emotion
- They want case studies, guarantees, and data
- They often delay decisions until they've "done more research"

Buyer Strategy:
- **Provide structure:** Use a clear, step-by-step explanation of your offer.
- **Show your receipts:** Use numbers, timelines, and proven outcomes.
- **Give them space:** Don't rush them, send detailed follow-ups instead.
- **Address risk upfront:** Show you've thought through the "what ifs."

Tip: Let them process. Follow up with a thoughtful summary email that recaps everything with bullet points and logical next steps.

You win with this buyer by being meticulous. They're looking for a reason to trust you, and they find that in your preparation, consistency, and knowledge.

3.   The Emotional Buyer: The Heart-Led Connector

This buyer is driven by feelings, relationships, and how a product or service aligns with their personal values or aspirations. Emotional buyers often purchase based on how they feel about you and your brand.

Key Traits: Intuitive, empathetic, relational, values-driven
Primary Question: "Does this feel right and align with who I am?"

They buy based on connection and vision. For them, trust and alignment matter more than details.

How to Spot Them:
They talk about their feelings or vision
They seek connection and ask personal questions
They respond well to storytelling
They often use phrases like "This just feels right" or "It speaks to me"

Buyer Strategy:
* **Lead with empathy:** Ask about their "why," not just their "what."
* **Use stories:** Testimonials and transformation journeys resonate most.
* **Emphasise shared values:** Showcase purpose, mission, and meaning.
* **Be vulnerable:** Authenticity builds deep trust.

Tip: With emotional buyers, presence is everything. Don't rush - make them feel seen and safe.

4.   The Logical Buyer: The Balanced Evaluator

Logical buyers are a blend of analytical and emotional, they value facts, but they also care about how a decision fits into their overall life or business strategy. They appreciate a well-structured presentation that speaks to both the head and the heart.

Key Traits: Objective, practical, even-keeled, solution-oriented
Primary Question: "Does this make sense overall?"

Logical buyers weigh both sides: emotion and evidence. They want clarity and common sense in the path forward.

How to Spot Them:

- They ask both data-driven and personal questions
- They balance scepticism with curiosity
- They tend to summarise what you've said for clarity
- They use phrases like "That makes sense" or "Walk me through it"

Buyer Strategy:
- Balance head and heart: Present logical steps with human benefits.
- Create a framework: Give them a roadmap with checkpoints.
- Ask reflective questions: Help them weigh pros and cons.
- Invite collaboration: Make it a partnership, not a pitch.

Tip: This buyer appreciates a structured process and open dialogue. Be organised, but warm.

Mirroring and Matching: The Secret Sauce

Once you identify your buyer's style, the next step is to meet them where they are. This is where mirroring and matching come in - powerful tools of connection rooted in psychology.

Mirroring means subtly reflecting the body language, tone, and pace of your prospect. Matching involves speaking in a way that aligns with their communication style.

For example:
- If a dominant buyer speaks fast and to the point - mirror their pace and tone.
- If an emotional buyer is expressive and warm - match their energy and openness.
- If an analytical buyer asks detailed questions - respond with thoughtful, precise answers.

Putting It All Together: The Buyer Match Matrix

Here's a quick reference to align your strategy:

BUYER TYPE	LEAD WITH	COMMUNICATION STYLE	TRUST TRIGGER
Dominant	Results & Impact	Direct, Decisive	Confidence & Efficiency
Analytical	Data & Process	Detailed, Methodical	Logic, Proof, Preparation
Emotional	Vision & Connection	Warm, Story-Driven	Authenticity & Empathy
Logical	Clarity & Structure	Balanced, Reflective	Simplicity & Thoughtfulness

Advanced Strategy: Mirroring, Matching, and Messaging

Once you›ve identified your buyer type, deepen the connection with conscious communication:

Mirroring: Subtly reflect their energy, language, and body language.
Matching: Align your tone, pace, and focus to match their rhythm.
Messaging: Tailor your language. For example:

- To Dominant buyers, say: "This strategy will accelerate your growth."
- To Analytical buyers, say: "Based on these numbers, here's the logical next step."
- To Emotional buyers, say: "This aligns beautifully with your values and purpose."
- To Logical buyers, say: "Here's a practical plan that fits your goals."

It's Not About Selling – It's About Seeing

When you know your buyer, you stop "pitching" and start partnering. This is the difference between transactional selling and transformational service.

Remember, everyone wants to feel understood. When you communicate in a way that matches how they think, feel, and decide, you create instant trust.

And trust is the real currency in sales.

So, the next time you're in a conversation, ask yourself:

"What matters most to this person, and how can speak their language?" When you do that, you'll stop chasing sales… and start creating success that feels good on both sides.

This doesn't mean being inauthentic. It means being intentional. When you match someone's style, you build trust faster because people feel safe when they sense familiarity.

It's Not Manipulation – It's Service

Let's be clear: tailoring your approach is not about manipulating people. It's about serving them in the way they best receive support. The greatest salespeople are not chameleons, they are mirrors. They reflect the buyer's needs, values, and language to create a bridge of understanding. When you take the time to understand who's in front of you, everything changes. Your conversations become more fluid. Your prospects feel seen. And most importantly, your service becomes more meaningful.

So, the next time you speak to a potential client, pause and ask yourself:

Who is this person, and how do they make decisions?

Then adjust your approach accordingly.

Understanding Instincts, Energy, and Human Connection

Here's the truth: every buyer, regardless of background, personality, or position, has an innate, almost primal instinct to get the best deal possible. It's a survival-level programming passed down through generations. Deep within all of us is that medieval instinct whispering, "Get the best price. Get the best value. Don't get ripped off." It's not personal. It's psychology. Now, as the seller, your job is to guide them toward a decision that aligns with their goals, and yes, to close the sale. But that's not about manipulation or pressure. It's about connection. It's about serving. And that requires something far more powerful than a pitch: presence.

Sales is an energetic exchange. Buyers are constantly sizing you up, sometimes with words, often without. There can be a disconnect between what they say and how they act. They may play hard to get or pretend they're not interested, while their body language tells a different story. And if you're paying attention, you'll see the truth before they even say a word. That's why face-to-face interaction, whether in person or via video, is so vital. When someone sees your face, hears your voice, watches your expressions, senses your tonality and energy, they're far more likely to trust you. You become congruent. Real. Human. And we trust what feels human.

Let me ask you something: when you've met someone face-to-face - shaken their hand, looked them in the eye, shared a laugh or a story - don't you trust them more? Aren't you more likely to open up to them, even buy from them? Of course you are. That's the power of true connection. And in today's digital world, with Zoom, WhatsApp, Teams, FaceTime - there's no excuse not to create that connection.

Because here's the danger: without the visual, without the tone, without the body language, you're guessing. A text message, email, or even a phone call without nuance leaves room for misinterpretation. You can't see the raised eyebrow, the nervous twitch, the crossed arms, the forced smile. And as a seller, these are your signals, they tell you how to move, when to push, when to pause, when to lean in, and when to back off.

Which brings me to the heart of buyer strategy: your energy must match and mirror theirs, without losing your own authenticity.

If you walk into a conversation bouncing like Tigger on espresso, but your prospect is calm, introverted, and reserved, it's going to feel off. Energetically, you're on different frequencies. So, what happens? Disconnection. Resistance. They check out. That doesn't mean you change who you are. But great sellers - authentic, heart-led sellers, are aware. You shift your delivery without compromising your truth. You soften your tone. Slow your pace. Pull out the calmer version of yourself that allows that buyer to feel safe, seen, and respected. Then, once you've matched their energy, you lead - gradually lifting the tempo, raising the energy, and guiding them upward with you.

People don't buy when they're overwhelmed. They buy when they feel understood.

So be fluid. Be like water, as Bruce Lee said. Go in without a predetermined outcome. Let go of assumptions, especially ones built from past sales calls or rejections. Each conversation is a new moment. A new human. A new possibility. Enter with curiosity, empathy, and a genuine desire to serve, not to sell.

Now, let's go deeper. People give objections all the time. "It's not the right time." "I need to speak to my partner." "It's too expensive." Nine times out of ten, these are reflexes, lines they've heard, absorbed, and repeated without thinking. So, your job is to lovingly, respectfully challenge those lines. Not by bulldozing through them, but by asking powerful questions that reveal the truth.

"What do you mean by that?"

"Can you help me understand that a little more?"

"Is that the real reason, or is there something else?"

These questions bring clarity. They peel back the layers of programmed responses and get to the real fear, doubt, or limiting belief holding them back. And once you're there, once you're speaking to the truth, not the surface-level story, you can lead them to the solution with compassion and confidence. Remember, people want to be understood. They want to feel that you "get them." When they feel that from you, when your language matches theirs, when your energy aligns, when your curiosity feels genuine, that›s when they trust. That's when they open up. That's when they say yes.

Because sales isn't about closing deals. It's about opening relationships. So, listen closely. Match their tone. Mirror their pace. Tune into the words they use. Pick up on the subtle cues. Challenge the clichés. Stay present. Be curious. Be human.

Be the kind of person you'd want to buy from.

Atlas
Deep Dive into The Buyer Strategy: Understanding the Real Person Behind the Purchase

Now that we›ve explored how to identify buyer types and how to communicate effectively with them, the next essential step in your buyer strategy is to truly understand the human being behind the purchase. We're not talking about surface-level chatter here - we're talking about the real person. The heart. The soul. The story. The why.

Ask Better Questions, Get Better Connections

One of the most powerful ways to connect and serve someone is to ask the questions that nobody else dares to ask. The kind of questions that go under the hood and reveal the truth.
Start with:

*   Why did you start your business?
*   What was your motivation?
*   Why is that important to you?
*   What's your real goal?
*   What does success actually look like for you?

Every time you're on a sales call - whether it's on Zoom, in person, or over the phone - this is the gold. These aren't just sales questions. These are human questions. When you ask them with genuine care and attention, people will open up.

Here's the secret: People love to talk about themselves. It's human nature. But they only do it when someone creates a safe space to do so. Your role as a heart-centred entrepreneur or sales professional is to be that space.

By asking the right questions, you're not just collecting data - you're building trust, connection, and rapport. You're signalling, «I see you. I care about you. I want to understand you.»

Identify the Pain to Provide the Path

Once you've uncovered their goals, the next step is to dig deeper:

*   What challenges are you currently facing?
*   What's the one thing you need to sort out right now?
*   What's keeping you stuck?

This is where the pain lives. And where there's pain, there's also an opportunity for transformation - if you listen carefully and respond with empathy.

And once you've identified the pain, don't stop there:

- What have you tried so far?
- What actions have you taken to solve this?
- What results did those actions get you?

Now you're building a timeline. You're uncovering commitment, patterns, frustrations, and real-life effort. You're learning where they've been, and - most importantly - where they want to go.

Get to the Core Beliefs

The next layer is perhaps the most important: beliefs. Because if someone's stuck, it's not always because of a lack of strategy - it's often because of a limiting belief they're carrying.

- What do they believe about success?
- What do they believe about salespeople?
- What do they believe about themselves?
- Where did those beliefs come from?
- What story have they been telling themselves?

This part is vital, because if you want someone to buy from you, they need to believe three things:

1. They can trust you.
2. Your offer works.
3. They are capable of getting results.

If one of those is missing, the sale will stall - guaranteed.

So, your role is not just to sell. Your role is to serve, to shift stories, and to show them what's truly possible.

Use Case Studies to Shift Belief

Once you've uncovered their limiting beliefs, meet them with a mirror - not a lecture. This is where storytelling becomes your best friend.

Tell them a story about a past client who had the same belief, the same challenge, the same pain - and show them how that person moved from stuck to successful using your product or service. This isn't about bragging; it's about bridging the gap between belief and possibility.

This is how you shift mindset in real-time, during the conversation. This is how you inspire someone to say yes with confidence.

Handle Objections Before They Arise

When you ask deep questions early and often, something amazing happens you eliminate objections before they even show up. Instead of scrambling at the end to justify your offer, you›re already integrating their pain, their beliefs, and their dreams into your solution.

They don't feel "sold to." They feel understood.

This Is How Lifelong Clients Are Made

When you ask better questions and connect from the heart, you're not just closing a deal - you're opening a relationship. You're building what I call a "Lifer." A client for life.

And it all starts with that first moment, that first connection, that first choice to care enough to go deeper than the usual script.

Sales isn't about being pushy, persuasive, or perfect. Sales is about being present. About being attractive, not in a superficial way, but in your energy - your emotional hygiene, your mindset, your intention. When you show up with clarity, confidence, curiosity, and care... that is attractive. That's what magnetises people to you.

A Final Thought on Presence and Energy
Let's get real for a moment. When someone meets you - whether they're aware of it or not - they're sizing you up instantly. Your posture, your eye contact, your tone, your energy. It's primal. And it matters.

So, before you go into any sales conversation, ask yourself:

Am I present?
Am I grounded?
Am I emotionally available?
Am I ready to serve, not sell?

Because when you are, that energy speaks louder than any pitch.

And if you've ever walked away from a store or a conversation where you wanted to buy - but didn't - it's probably because the seller didn't connect with you. They didn't see you. They didn't ask the questions that mattered. Don't let that be you.

KEY TAKEAWAY:

To master buyer strategy, you must master the art of deep understanding. Get under the hood. Ask better questions. Uncover beliefs. Eliminate objections early. Shift stories. And most of all - connect with people like their future depends on it. Because it does.

Belief Blocks the Silent Saboteurs of Sales

Before you even get on a call, send a proposal, or pitch your offer, your beliefs are already doing the talking. Your beliefs shape your energy. Your energy shapes your communication. And your communication shapes your results. Many heart-centered entrepreneurs struggle with sales not because they lack skill—but because they carry subconscious belief blocks that sabotage their success.

Here are a few of the most common:

"I'm not good at sales"
You've absorbed the idea that selling is a personality trait instead of a skill. This belief shuts you down before you even try.

"I don't want to come across as pushy"
If you believe sales equals pressure, you'll do everything to avoid the close, even when the client is ready to buy.

"People can't afford me"
This often reflects your relationship with money, not your client's. It causes you to undercharge, over give, or talk people out of a sale.

"I need to prove myself first"
Perfectionism in disguise. This block keeps you trapped in preparation, instead of trusting that you're already enough to serve powerfully.

The key is this - Your beliefs create your sales reality.

To shift your results, you must become conscious of the stories you're telling yourself and then choose new ones.

Ask yourself:

- What do I believe about money and sales?
- Where did that belief come from?
- Is it absolutely true?
- What would I rather believe instead?

Affirm:
"I sell with integrity. I serve with heart. My offer is valuable, and the right clients are ready to say yes."

Observe: Mastering the Art of Sales Awareness

Sales isn't just about talking. It's about watching, listening, and feeling. One of the most powerful things you can do in a sales conversation is to shift from performance mode to observer mode.
You're not here to impress. You're here to tune in.

Observation opens the door to deep empathy and powerful connection. It allows you to:

- Pick up on non-verbal cues (hesitation, excitement, confusion)
- Sense emotional shifts (when a person leans in or pulls away)
- Hear what's not being said (the real concern behind a surface-level question)

And most importantly, it helps you know when to lean in and when to hold space. A great salesperson is a great detective. You're gathering clues with every response, every pause, every question.

Try this:

In your next call, mentally step back. Watch their tone, their eyes (if on video), their energy. What's really going on underneath their words?

Observation also means watching yourself:

- Do you rush to fill the silence?
- Do you jump in to defend your price?
- Do you tighten up when they ask about cost?

Your own body language, tone, and presence are powerful tools. Observe them. Own them.

Objection Handling: The Heart-Centered Way

Here's the truth about objections:

Objections are not rejections. They are invitations for deeper connection.

When someone says, "I can't afford it", they're rarely talking about their bank balance. They're talking about trust, in the offer, in you, or in

89

themselves. A heart-centered entrepreneur doesn't bulldoze objections. They explore them, with curiosity and compassion.

Here's a powerful 3-step framework to respond to any objection:

1.   Acknowledge - Let them feel seen. Never argue or dismiss.
 "I completely understand - that makes total sense."

2.   Ask - Dig deeper with loving curiosity.
"Can I ask, is it the investment itself, or uncertainty about the result?"

3.   Align - Reaffirm your role and realign them with their vision.
"I'm here to help you get the outcome you want. If money weren't a factor, would this be the right next step for you?"

This opens the space for truth to emerge, often it›s not about the money at all. It's about fear. Doubt. Timing. Self-belief. And when you handle that with love instead of pressure, you build trust. That's what closes sales.

Remember: objections are part of the journey, not a signal to retreat. Lean in with love.

Manifest the Key Result: Sales from Soul Alignment

Now, let's bring it all together.
You've understood the buyer's psychology.
You've worked through your belief blocks.
You've shown up with awareness, listened deeply, and responded with heart.

Now, it's time to call in the result - not with force, but with alignment. Manifestation in sales isn't just spiritual - it's strategic.

It's about:

•   Speaking directly to the outcome your client desires
•   Offering with confidence and conviction
•   Trusting in the value you provide
•   Letting go of attachment to the outcome

You are not here to convince - You are here to invite.

When your energy, words, and intentions are aligned with service, sales become natural. Joyful. Magnetic. Your ideal clients feel that energy.

They say yes, not just to your offer, but to themselves. This is the power of heart-centered sales.

You don't hustle to win.

You hold space for everyone to win.

Selling is not something you do TO someone. It's something you do FOR them and WITH them. When you remove the pressure, reframe objections, and shift your internal stories, sales stop being scary. They start being sacred. This is how we serve. This is how we sell. This is how we lead.

Delivering a Sales training session

On stage & at my 3 day heart of the sale training

![marcus elwell — SALES MINDSET TRANSFORMATION]

www.marcus@marcuselwell.com

Check out my website for

details of my services

marcus
elwell
SALES MINDSET TRANSFORMATION

CHAPTER FOUR

METHODICAL SERVICE

Strategies for Consistent and Effective Delivery

If there's one truth, we've established so far, it's this: people buy from people. And not just from anyone, but from those who understand them, respect them, and show up with authenticity, empathy, and integrity. The best sales conversations don't feel like sales at all. They feel like two people connecting on a human level. But connection alone isn't enough. Connection without structure leads to confusion. Empathy without clarity leads to stagnation, and compassion without consistency, that's where potential deals fall through the cracks. So, once you've earned someone's attention and opened the door to trust, what comes next? Now we transition from the art of sales, the emotional, relational, and psychological to the science of service. This next chapter is about strategy. It's about having a method, because even though every client is different, your process shouldn't be. The delivery of your service, and your ability to guide someone from first contact to final agreement, requires a repeatable, reliable framework. This is where we move from understanding people to serving people well.

In Chapter 4, we'll break down what I call Methodical Service. It's a step-by-step approach to ensure every person you engage with receives the same level of excellence, care, and clarity. It's not about robotic routines. It's about intentional actions that build on the human connection you've established, so that trust turns into transformation. Think of this chapter as your operations manual for the service side of sales. You've done the internal work. You've developed emotional intelligence. Now it's time to systemise your success. Let's dive into Methodical Service and learn how to turn meaningful connections into consistent conversions.

We'll walk through seven critical elements:

1. **Treating Them Like Family** – Don't treat your clients like a money symbol but as how you would want your family to be treated.

In a world of scripts, strategies, and sales funnels, we sometimes forget the most potent strategy of all: love. Not the soft, fluffy kind that shrinks back when things get uncomfortable—but the intentional, practical, show-up-every-time kind of love that family **should** represent. The kind that sees people, not prospects. That's the heartbeat of Methodical Service: consistent, intentional excellence, grounded in how you'd want your own family to be treated.

Think about it. If your mother called you asking for help navigating a difficult decision, would you rush her off the phone or flood her with jargon she doesn't understand? If your brother needed guidance on something he didn't fully grasp, would you manipulate his fear to push him toward a sale? Of course not. You'd slow down. You'd listen. You'd break it down clearly, respectfully, lovingly. You'd serve.

That's the golden standard.

When you adopt a family-first mindset in your methodical service approach, every touchpoint becomes sacred. It's not just about being friendly or polite. It's about being responsible for how people feel after engaging with you. Whether it's your discovery call, onboarding email, proposal follow-up, or the moment they say "yes" - each step should be delivered with the same excellence, empathy, and clarity you'd give to someone you truly care about.

Here's the kicker though - this kind of service can't be reserved only for your "ideal clients" or the ones who can pay top dollar.

Methodical Service means everyone gets the full-course meal, not just the VIPs. Everyone gets the warmth, the clarity, the dignity. Even the ones who say no. Even the ones who ghost. Because when you build a business culture where excellence is the *default setting*, you attract the kind of relationships that lead to legacy, not just sales.

Clarity at Every Stage – Confusion is the silent killer of trust. Treat clients like family by demystifying your process. Avoid buzzwords. Use plain language. Repeat if needed. When they walk away from a conversation with you, they should feel lighter, not more burdened.

Consistency Is Kindness – You wouldn›t ignore your cousin's text for a week, then pop up asking for a favour if you do, you are on your way to damaging your relationship with them or you have already been marked. Be prompt. Be reliable. Build systems that help you follow up with grace and regularity. Professionalism is just consistency with heart.

Personalisation, Not Just Automation – Systems are essential, but soul must lead. Add human touches to your follow-ups. Mention their goals, acknowledge their concerns, and don't let them feel like one of many in a spreadsheet.

Boundaries Build Trust – Even family needs boundaries. You don't have to over give or self-abandon to prove you care. Structure your offerings and availability with wisdom. Honor your time and teach others to do the same. That's a form of service too.

Ask Better Questions – When you treat people like family, you don't assume - you inquire. Ask deeper questions that show genuine curiosity, not just surface-level interest in the sale. Learn about what matters to them. Their "why" is your compass.

Follow Through Like It's Your Name on the Line – Because it is. Deliver what you said you would. Then go a little further. That extra check-in, that resource you didn't have to send - that's what separates a transaction from a transformation.

In this heart-led, methodical approach to service, you don't just close deals - you open doors. You create a ripple effect where clients feel honoured, not handled. Where they refer you without being asked. Where they come back, not because you pushed them, but because you pulled them in with integrity and care.

Treating them like family doesn't mean being unprofessional. It means being personable with purpose. You become the steady, trustworthy guide who doesn't just want their money—you want their success, their peace of mind, and their long-term transformation.

That's Methodical Service. And that's the heart of the sale.

2. **Establish Rapport** – Going beyond surface-level connection and building emotional trust early.

The first step in any heart-centred sales conversation is to establish rapport not as a tactic, but as a sincere act of connection. Rapport isn't about scripted small talk or surface-level flattery; it's about creating a safe, respectful space where the other person feels seen, heard, and valued. When someone feels emotionally at ease, their defences drop, and their openness rises, and that's when meaningful conversation begins. Building rapport starts with presence. When you're fully present, listening with genuine curiosity, not waiting to speak or thinking about your pitch, you communicate respect. Mirroring their energy, pace, and tone in an authentic way also helps foster subconscious alignment. This isn't manipulation; it's about attuning to their rhythm without abandoning your own. Use their name naturally, offer warm eye contact, and lead with curiosity rather than an agenda. Ask thoughtful, open-ended questions like, "What inspired you to explore this?" or "What would the ideal outcome look like for you?" These questions invite them to open up and invite you in. When rapport is built on authenticity, not performance, trust becomes the foundation. And trust is where all great service - and every lasting sale - begins.

3. **Needs Analysis** – Asking the right questions to uncover real desires and hidden pain points

Once rapport is established and you've listened actively, it's time to move into a focused needs analysis, the heart of truly understanding how you can serve the person in front of you. This isn't about pushing an agenda or rushing toward a sale. It's about creating space for exploration. Through thoughtful, open-ended questions, you gently guide the conversation to uncover their current situation, their struggles, their goals, and what's standing in the way. Questions like "What would success look like for you?" or "What's the biggest challenge you're facing right now?" invite deep reflection. As they share, pay attention to their tone, their energy, and the emotions behind their words. Don't just capture data, tune into desires, fears, and values. A great needs analysis is rooted in genuine curiosity and the belief that the better you understand their world, the better you can serve them. This phase builds on trust and lays the foundation for aligned, ethical recommendations. When done with integrity, it never feels invasive, it feels like care. You're not diagnosing to sell; you're discovering how, or if, you can truly help.

4. **Guide Them Through the Process** – Leading, not pushing. Making their next step feel safe and natural.

With a deep understanding of their needs now in hand, you can move naturally into positioning the solution, but this isn't about pitching. It's about reflecting on what they've shared and showing how your offering aligns with their goals, values, and current challenges. Begin by summarising what you heard: "From what you've shared, it sounds like you're looking for..." This demonstrates that you've been present, not just listening, but truly understanding. Then, connect the dots between their needs and your solution. This isn't about listing features - it's about illuminating outcomes. How will their life or business be better after working with you? Paint that picture clearly and authentically, focusing on the transformation rather than the transaction. Use language that matches their emotional tone, and only position solutions that are genuinely in their best interest. When done with heart, this step doesn't feel like selling, it feels like offering a lifeline, a pathway forward. And when the solution is positioned in this grounded, caring way, it becomes an invitation, not a pitch.

5. **Address the Pre-Objective** – Uncovering unspoken fears or hesitations before they derail the conversation.

After positioning the solution with clarity and care, pause, don't rush to the close. Instead, create space for your prospective client to process what they've heard. This is the pre-objection stage, and it's often overlooked. It's the moment where they begin internally weighing everything you've shared against their fears, doubts, and past experiences. Your job here is not to convince, but to hold space. Watch their body language, tone of voice, and energy. Ask, "How does that feel to you?" or "What's coming up for you as you hear this?" These gentle, open-ended questions show that you're still prioritising service over selling. Often, this moment reveals unspoken objections before they're ever voiced, things like uncertainty about timing, confidence in themselves, or fear of making the wrong decision. By addressing these emotional undercurrents with empathy and presence, you disarm resistance before it hardens. You're not pushing them into a 'yes', you're walking beside them toward a decision they feel empowered to make. And that is what transforms a sales conversation into a sacred exchange of trust.

6. **Gain Their Agreement** – Ethically aligning their needs with your solution and inviting them to move forward.

Gaining the client's agreement is a pivotal moment in the heart-centred sales process, it's where alignment becomes action. After you've guided them through a values-based conversation, uncovered their true needs, and addressed any lingering hesitations, it's time to invite a decision. But instead of pushing or convincing, you simply reflect the journey you've taken together and hold space for a "yes" that comes from clarity, not coercion. Use language that feels collaborative and affirming, like: "It sounds like this solution meets what you're looking for, how does that feel to you?" or "Are you ready to take this next step together?" This approach honours their autonomy and emphasises that this is a mutual decision. When they agree, acknowledge their commitment with warmth and confidence: "That's a powerful decision, I'm honoured to support you." This isn't about closing a sale, it's about opening a relationship, built on trust, transformation, and aligned intention.

7. **Execute** – Delivering on your promise with clarity, precision, and a commitment to excellence.

Executing the agreement means delivering on your promise with clarity, precision, and a wholehearted commitment to excellence. This stage is where trust is truly built and solidified. Be transparent about what the client can expect next, outline the steps clearly, set realistic timelines, and communicate openly throughout the process. Follow through consistently, keeping the client informed and engaged every step of the way. Excellence isn't just about meeting expectations; it's about exceeding them wherever possible, showing your dedication to their success and satisfaction. When you deliver with integrity and reliability, you not only fulfil your promise but also create a foundation for long-term relationships, referrals, and ongoing collaboration. This is where service meets action, and the heart-centred sales approach comes full circle.

Dealing with the Elephant in the Room

Let's talk about it. You know...the big, Gray, unspoken, slightly awkward elephant in the room. The one wearing a name tag that says:

"Are they going to try to sell me something?"

It shows up at free webinars, workshops with "limited seats," and events where the host charges little to nothing - only for the audience to be blindsided with a sales pitch halfway through, feeling like they've just been baited into a timeshare presentation rather than a transformation experience.

Let me be clear: that is not the method of a heart-centred, service-led entrepreneur.

I don't believe in tricking people into trust.

Manipulation may move a few products, but it will never build a movement.

In my world - and in yours, if you›re committed to authentic selling - the elephant gets invited to the front row, offered a snack, and formally introduced at the very start. Why? Because integrity doesn't hide behind a curtain waiting for the right moment to jump out. It walks in first, looks you in the eye, and tells the truth.

So, here's how I do it:

From the outset, I let people know that at some point, I'll be making an offer. Not with pressure, not with shame, not with gimmicks or countdown clocks or fabricated scarcity - but with clarity, confidence, and choice.

I tell them, "I'm going to give you so much value during our time together, you'll leave better than you came. And if, by the end, you feel like you'd like to go deeper and continue this journey with me, I'll let you know how. No pressure - just presence, and a clear next step if it fits."

That kind of transparency disarms suspicion and builds trust. People respect you more when you're upfront. And here's the twist: being honest about the offer doesn't repel people. It relaxes them. Why? Because they no longer have to second-guess your motives. They can stop trying to read between the lines and simply receive.

Let's be honest - most people don't mind being offered help. They just don't like being ambushed by it.

When you bring the offer out of the shadows and into the light with love, excellence, and timing, you're not selling - you're serving with clarity. You're saying, "This is the table I've set. If you're hungry, you're welcome to eat. But you're not obligated to do anything except receive what's been freely given."

There is nothing manipulative about an offer.
There is nothing shameful about extending an invitation.
What's wrong is when that invitation comes cloaked in trickery, coated in fear, or delivered with the tone of desperation instead of dignity.

In your methodical service model, dealing with the elephant in the room is step one in making sure every person feels safe, seen, and respected - whether they say yes, no, or not yet. So go ahead, mention the elephant. Name it. Smile at it. Because once it's out in the open, you've cleared the space for authenticity, freedom, and genuine connection - and that is where true sales happen.

To wrap up this chapter, it's essential to recognise that authentic selling is much more than just closing a deal, it's about building a foundation of trust and mutual respect. When you take the time to establish genuine rapport, you create a safe space where your client feels heard and valued. Moving into a detailed needs analysis allows you to uncover their true motivations, challenges, and desires, ensuring that your solution is not just a product, but a perfect fit for their unique situation. Addressing objections isn't a hurdle to avoid, but an opportunity to deepen understanding and reinforce your commitment to their success. By handling concerns with empathy and transparency, you shift the conversation from scepticism to confidence. Gaining their agreement becomes a natural next step, a mutual decision grounded in clarity and alignment rather than pressure.

Finally, executing your promise with clarity, precision, and a commitment to excellence is where the true power of heart-centred sales shines. It's in delivering on what you've promised, that trust transforms into loyalty. Every interaction is a chance to demonstrate your integrity and dedication, reinforcing the relationship and paving the way for ongoing collaboration.

Embracing this process transforms sales from a transactional exchange into a meaningful service. It positions you not just as a seller, but as a trusted advisor and partner. As you continue to refine and practice these principles, you'll find that your business thrives not only through increased sales but through deeper connections, authentic influence, and lasting impact.

This is the heart of the sale -where everybody wins.

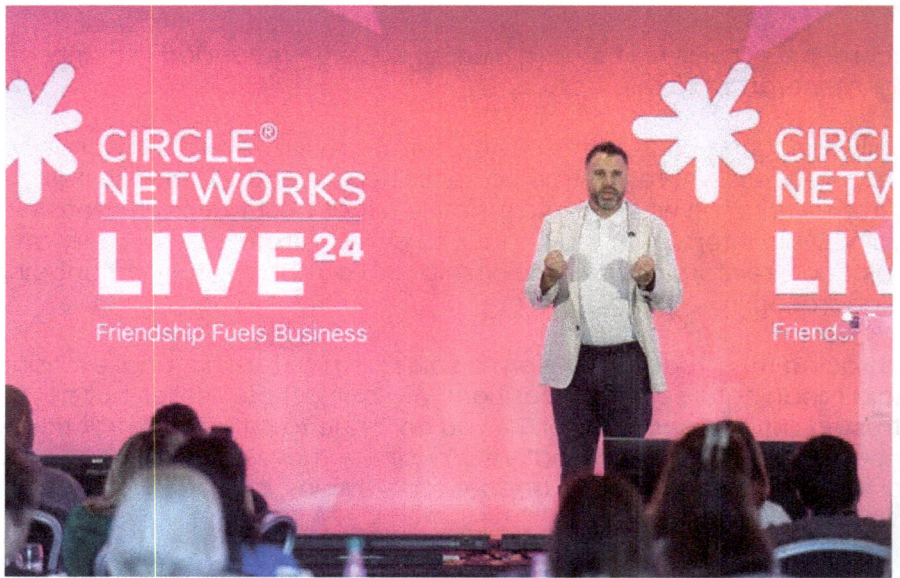

Speaking at the Circle Networks Live 24

*With my great friend & Supporter
Jason finishing our first triathlon*

CHAPTER FIVE

CRAFTING AUTHENTIC CONNECTIONS

Building Relationships Through Service

It was one of those classic British summer days. A little cloud cover, but that stubborn, hopeful optimism in the air - the kind that makes you believe the sun's going to break through at any moment.
I stood there, 23 years old, in a London auction room, heart pounding, palms sweaty, about to bid on a piece of land that had once been a run-down petrol station. Not just any petrol station - this was the one I used to pass on my way to school. And if I'm being brutally honest, I'd even nicked a cheeky ice cream from there once or twice. (Look, don't judge - I didn't know better back then.)

But now?

That same boy was standing in a suit, in a room full of seasoned investors, about to make a play for that exact plot.

"Going once... going twice... SOLD - to the boys from Hollywood!"

That was us - my brother and me. Shaking. Laughing. Slightly terrified. Completely out of our depth. But absolutely all in.

We didn't have all the answers. We didn't know exactly how it would work. But what we did have was belief, vision, and an unshakable commitment to go full throttle. We wrote the cheque for 10% on the spot, got handed a cigar and a glass of red, and were told to breathe.

Over the next few years, we transformed that petrol station into a two-storey, purpose-built tile and bathroom showroom. It was bold. It was big. And it was ours.

But then came 2008. The economy crashed. The phones stopped ringing. The customers vanished. We went from busy and booming to dead quiet - overnight. I looked around at my staff, my business partner, our orders board... empty. It was like the carpet had been ripped from under us.

You see, when people look at me now and say, "Wow, Marcus, you built two 7-figure businesses," that's true. But what they don't see is the cost. The stress. The sleepless nights. The times I stared down the barrel and thought I might lose it all. They don't see the inner battles - the financial strain, the mental pressure, the relationship fallout.

And yet... it all taught me something invaluable.

The businesses I built didn't survive because I was the smartest guy in the room. They didn't thrive because I had the slickest pitch. They succeeded because, through it all, I stayed true to one core principle:

I always led with heart. I wore it on my sleeve. I didn't fake it. I didn't play the big man or pretend I had all the answers. I just showed up as my real, raw, honest self - especially in the tough conversations.

Because here's the truth: if you want to build real relationships that drive real business, you've got to stop hiding. You've got to stop dancing around the elephant in the room. You've got to serve, not sell - and that starts with courageous conversations.

So let me ask you:

When was the last time you went all in?

When was the last time you had a conversation with a potential customer and really listened - not to respond, not to pitch, but to connect?

If you want more conversions, you need more connection. And that doesn't happen by playing nice and fluffy. That happens when you show up with integrity and ask the hard questions:

- "What's holding you back from making a decision?"
- "Is it really about the money, or is there something else?"
- "What needs to happen for us to do business together today?"

These questions don't just uncover objections - they uncover truth. And truth builds trust.

Here's the secret: even when a prospect says no, if you've asked with heart, they'll remember you. Because you didn't just try to close a deal - you opened a relationship.

And that's what Chapter 5 is all about: creating authentic connections by being willing to get real, get raw, and ask the questions others shy away from.

Not everyone will buy from you. That's okay.

But they should all walk away knowing you saw them, heard them, and honoured them with honesty. When you serve people like that, your reputation becomes your marketing. Word spreads. Doors open. And your business grows - organically, powerfully, and with integrity.

Let's dive in.

Now it is all about the money you›ve left on the table, and how to go back and get it. I'm not talking about theory or concepts here. I'm talking about real, tangible results you can access right now. This is the part of the book where we start activating 'sales quick wins' - opportunities for revenue that already exist within your business, just waiting for you to take action. Often, we think we need more leads, more visibility, or another launch to hit our goals. But the truth? You're likely sitting on a goldmine already. Think about the leads you've quoted who didn't buy. The past clients who loved working with you but haven't heard from you since. The warm conversations that fizzled out before the close. These are the people we're going to revisit. These are the relationships we're going to reignite.

Let's start with the most overlooked and underutilised segment of your sales process: your lost quotes.

Let's dive in.

Now it is all about the money you›ve left on the table, and how to go back and get it. I'm not talking about theory or concepts here. I'm talking about real, tangible results you can access right now. This is the part of the book where we start activating 'sales quick wins' - opportunities for revenue that already exist within your business, just waiting for you to take action. Often, we think we need more leads, more visibility, or another launch to hit our goals. But the truth? You're likely sitting on a goldmine already. Think about the leads you've quoted who didn't buy. The past clients who loved working with you but haven't heard from you since. The warm conversations that fizzled out before the close. These are the people we're going to revisit. These are the relationships we're going to reignite.

Let's start with the most overlooked and underutilised segment of your sales process: your lost quotes.

Start by scanning through them. Pull up your CRM, your emails, your DMs, wherever your prospects live, and look for those who received a quote but didn't go ahead. Now rate each one on a scale of one to ten. A "1" is ice cold, maybe they ghosted you and never replied. A "5" is lukewarm, you exchanged a few messages, but it just didn't go anywhere. A "10" is your sweet spot, people who had great rapport with you, said they were interested, and maybe even told you they were close… but didn't commit. Start with the tens. This is where the magic happens. These people liked you. They connected with your offer. They saw the value, but something, somewhere, got in the way. Your job now isn't to pressure them into a sale. It's to reconnect. It's to find out what shifted, what stalled, and whether there's still a need.

Next, check your timeline. When did you last speak to them? If it's been less than three months, that's perfect. It's still fresh. Don't assume their circumstances haven't changed. They may have just been overwhelmed. They may still need your help but haven't had the time or energy to revisit the decision. And even if it's been longer, six months or more, it's still worth exploring. Prioritise those who made you think, *"I can't believe they didn't go ahead."*

Now here's the part that separates heart-centred leaders from passive hopefuls: pick up the phone. Don't just email. Don't just send a DM. Call them. Let them hear your voice. That's how we cut through the noise and create authentic reconnection. Say something simple and direct: "Hey [Name], it's [Your Name]. I realised we never finished our conversation, and I just wanted to check in. Did you make a decision about the quote I sent?" No fluff. No weird buildup. Go straight in, and let it be about them. From there, recap your last interaction. Remind them of what you discussed and what they were considering. Be genuinely curious, ask them how they're doing. Where things are at. Whether they moved forward. And if they didn't, why not? What changed? What's holding them back now?

This is where you lean in. Don't let polite brush-offs end the conversation. If they tell you, it wasn't the right time or something came up, explore that. Ask what's shifted. Say, "That makes sense, can I ask, is this still something you want or need?" or "What would have made this a clear yes for you back then?" These questions help both of you gain clarity. If it turns out they're not your ideal client, that's a win too. Now you know. You've got closure. But if they are the right fit and it was just timing, uncertainty, or fear holding them back, this is your opportunity to guide them forward. Offer a bonus. Restructure the package. Present a fresh opportunity with a time-sensitive incentive. Not as a manipulation tactic, but as an invitation to act from a place of clarity.

Here›s the powerful part most people forget: even if they say no, ask for a referral. You've reconnected. You've provided value. Now ask, "If this isn't something you need right now, is there anyone in your network who might?" You'll be surprised how often they know someone. Even more powerful? Ask them to connect you directly, right then and there. Don't leave the door cracked open. Walk through it. Now, let's be real, objections will come up. Be ready for them. If it's price, can you offer a payment plan? If it's time, help them see the cost of staying stuck. If it's overwhelm, remind them you're not just selling them a service, you're supporting them through the process. Ask, "What would need to change for this to feel like a yes?" or "What's the impact of not doing this now?" Revisiting lost quotes isn't about being pushy. It's about being present. It's about showing up with care and clarity, ready to serve, ready to support. This is the work of a heart-led sales leader. And it's the work that will bring you not only more sales, but deeper relationships, greater trust, and a thriving community of aligned clients.

The truth is, we›re not going to suddenly have more time. If anything, life gets busier. That's just how it goes. So, if you're someone who keeps saying, "Once I get through this next thing, once I hit point C, then I'll be ready to get from A to B," let me stop you right there. No, now. The time is now. There's no better time than this moment, right here, right now. Stop waiting. Start moving and that brings us full circle, back to the power of follow-up and the heart of service. If you approach sales conversations with this strategy in mind, if you come armed with a clear process, then you can expect objections. But with the tools you're learning in this book, you'll also have the power to lovingly, empathetically challenge those objections. That's how you lead someone to commit and move forward with you.

Let me give you a real-life example to show just how powerful this can be. I once worked with a CBD company, one that specialised in topical solutions for pain relief and complex skin issues. They had sent a quote to a major retailer but never followed up. Nothing came of it, and they left the deal on the table. When I stepped in and implemented the exact strategy you're learning here, I rebuilt the connection with the buyer. It didn't happen overnight, it took a few calls over the course of about three months, but I wasn't there to close a deal. I was there to open *a relationship.*

Eventually, the follow-up paid off. That buyer placed a £35,000 order, one that repeated every quarter. What started as zero sales turned into a six-figure annual contract that's still going strong three years later.

All because of the follow-up. I answered her questions fully, helped her overcome hesitations, and took my time to serve, not sell.

Here's a pro tip: don't BS. Don't rush. Give the full, real answer, even if that means saying you don't know yet. Integrity matters. Your values matter. And trust me, people respect honesty. If someone asks a question and you don't have the answer, say so. Tell them, "I want to make sure I give you the most accurate information, so let me double-check and get back to you." That honesty builds trust, and trust builds long-term business. I did this myself during that CBD project. There were a couple of questions I thought I knew the answers to, but I double-checked and came back with the right answers. If I'd guessed and been wrong, she would've known, and that would've been game over. This brings us to another powerful sales quick win: past clients. These are people who already knew you, already trusted you - at least to some degree. So, the question is, how did you leave things with them? Rate each past client relationship from 1 to 10. One is awful, five is neutral, and anything between seven and ten is where your gold is. Focus there first.

Now ask: when did you last speak with them? If it's been less than three months, they probably still want you - they just haven't reached out because life gets in the way. Time is always a factor. If it's been more than three months, there's still opportunity - but you'll need to approach them with care and curiosity.

Start with the ones you can't believe you lost. Pick up the phone - don't email - and reconnect. Sure, you can use a WhatsApp voice note or another personal method, but your goal is to open the relationship again. Here's how you do it:

Start with a friendly reminder of who you are:
"Hi, it's Marcus from [Company]. We spoke a few months ago about [topic/product/service], and I realised I hadn't followed up with you, my bad on that. I just wanted to check in and see how things are going for you now. Are things better? Did you find a solution that's working?"

This isn't a sales call. It's a feedback call. Wear your relationship manager hat and get curious. Ask:
- What's changed since we last spoke?
- Did you end up going with someone else?
- If so, how's that working out?
- What would need to happen for us to work together again?

This is your chance to improve, your services, your delivery, your process. Own any mistakes. Ask for honest feedback. If they've moved on, find out why. If they're still stuck, offer to help. And then, when the moment's right, make an offer. Give them a reason to re-engage. Maybe it's a special incentive, a one-time deal, or a tailored package that makes it a no-brainer. And frame it with care. "You came to mind when we launched this new offer, I realised I might not have served you as well as I could have, and I'd love to change that."

Here's another example. I once worked with a marketing training company that wanted me to film their one-day event. I said, "Sure, but give me your old customer list." I called each person personally and showed them the love. I asked what they were up to, what results they'd seen, and what their experience had been. Some said they liked the offer, but it was too expensive. Others said they didn't get the follow-up they expected. Others said they loved the training but didn't feel cared for.

So, I asked: What needs to happen for us to work together again? And I listened, really listened. The result? We filled the event. It became a £20,000 day, and many of those attendees upgraded to a top-tier package, resulting in nearly £100,000 in total sales. All from a few follow-up calls.

Pro tip: the first sale is just the start. The real win comes from what happens next, how you nurture, serve, and convert again.

Of course, all of this only works if your mindset is right. And I get it, this is where most people trip up. When I say, "Pick up the phone," most people panic. They think, "Well, it's easy for you. You've done this a long time." But let me tell you: I'm no different than you. The only difference is that I've practiced, and I've made mindset my priority.

So, here's a mindset mantra: You're not annoying them until they tell you to f* off. And by the way, no one's ever said that to me. Not once.

Go for no. Don't take it personally. Challenge people lovingly. Serve them deeply. And yes, sometimes they're genuinely busy, so don't get discouraged when they ask you to call back. But when you do, book the next call. Don't leave it open-ended. Get their permission to follow up. Be bold.

Because if you don't follow up, you're not helping them. You're not solving their problem. And that, my friend, is a disservice.

Your job is to challenge with empathy, to lovingly push them toward the solution that helps them and supports you. That's service. That's sales.

Your challenge from this chapter? Go implement this.
- Don't just read it, do it. Pick up the phone.
- Reconnect with past clients.
- Reignite lost quotes.
- Listen deeply.
- Serve powerfully.
- Trust that the results will follow.

Before we proceed to the next chapter, let us look further at a few crucial elements that will enable you to craft authentic connections.

Contacts: Relationships Before Revenue
When was the last time you really looked at your contact list, not as a sales database, but as a collection of human beings you've crossed paths with? Every name in your system has a story. A reason you connected. Maybe it was at a networking event, maybe they downloaded a freebie, maybe they liked your post two years ago and ended up on your list. Either way, the connection already exists. It just needs to be reawakened.

For example, Lara, a virtual assistant coach, had over 1,000 contacts she hadn't emailed in nearly a year. She was worried people would unsubscribe or be annoyed if she suddenly reappeared in their inbox. Instead of sending a hard-sell campaign, we crafted a reintroduction series that focused on storytelling and care.

The first line of her email read:
"You may not remember me, but I haven't forgotten why I started this journey — to help women like you build freedom with a business that supports your life."

She shared her journey, what she'd learned, and offered a free planning session as a gift. The results? Over 60 sessions booked, 12 new clients signed, and dozens of replies simply saying, "Thank you for this message. I needed it."

Lesson: Your contacts are not cold leads. They're warm opportunities waiting for a human touch.

List (Quotes): Unfinished Conversations with Huge Potential

Every quote that hasn't converted is not a rejection, it's an open door. People get distracted. Budgets shift. Priorities change. But what doesn't change is the value you offer. The question is: are you courageous enough to follow up?

Take Naomi, a wedding photographer who had quoted 22 brides over the last year but only booked 8. We reviewed every single one of those quotes and noticed a pattern, most went cold after the initial quote with no follow-up strategy in place. We crafted a three-part sequence that reignited the conversation without pressure.

Here's a snippet of what we used:
"Hey [Name], I know wedding planning can be hectic, and I just wanted to check in to see if you found the right photographer for your big day. If not, I'd love to see how I can support you, even if that's just pointing you in the right direction."

That message booked her 3 new weddings in a single week. One client said she had intended to book her but got overwhelmed and simply forgot to reply.

Takeaway: A quote is a conversation. Don't leave it unfinished - gently walk it to the finish line.

3.Existing Clients Are Diamonds in the Dust
Your existing clients are sitting on a goldmine - not just for potential sales, but for insight, connection, and growth. But here's the question I want to ask you:
How many of your existing clients know what you do - fully?

I'm not talking about that one product or service they bought from you last year. I'm talking about everything, all the ways you can help, the offers you've added, the new results you're delivering. The truth is most of them don't know. Why? Because you think you've told them. But just because you know doesn't mean they understand it. This is where most entrepreneurs and sales professionals miss massive quick-win opportunities. They expect people to just get it, to remember them, to keep up with their content, to know what's available. But life is busy. Algorithms are noisy. Competitors are loud. And the moment you slip out of someone's sight, you're out of their mind, even if they love you. Here's what I want you to do. Start with your longest-standing clients, your account customers, the ones who've bought from you before.

Pick up the phone. Reintroduce yourself. Not with a hard pitch, but with genuine interest and clarity.

Ask: "Did you know I now offer [X]?"
"How have things been since we last worked together?"
"Who in your network might need help with [specific offer or solution]?"

For example, one of my clients, a branding consultant named Sarah, had worked with dozens of small businesses on logo design. But what her past clients didn't know was that she now offered full brand strategy, social media kits, and website audits. We got her on the phone with 10 former clients, just checking in, asking questions, and sharing updates. Four of them said the same thing: "Oh, I didn't know you did that! I've been thinking about rebranding."

That's what I mean by diamonds in the dust.
They›re right there, ready, valuable, familiar, just covered up by time, assumption, and silence.

Follow-Up Is Service, Not Sales Pressure
When you reach out to a past client, do it with the mindset of service, not sales. Your goal is to reconnect, to understand how they're doing, to find out if what you now offer could support where they're at. That's the shift, this isn't cold calling. These people already chose you once. That means trust has already been built. You're not pushing something on them, you're giving them a chance to say "yes" again.

Ask about their results. Ask what worked, what didn't. And be open to feedback. In fact, welcome it, even if it's uncomfortable. Because the minute you think you've cracked it and stop improving, you're moving backwards. Every conversation is a chance to listen, grow, and refine. If someone gives you constructive feedback, even if it feels a bit sharp, take a breath and say:

"Thank you. I appreciate that. I'll take it on board."

That level of humility and openness not only strengthens your relationship, but it also positions you as someone who cares more about service than ego, and that is what keeps clients coming back and referring others. Let's get real. There are people who love what you do… who just forgot. The noise of the market, the chaos of everyday life, and the constant targeting by your competitors means that even your best clients can lose focus and drift away.

Not because they're disloyal, but because they're human. Social media algorithms don't always show your content. Your emails might get buried. And if you don't personally show up now and then, you risk becoming invisible. Reopen conversations. Don't just post and pray. Message people. Call them. Voice-note them. Be human. Be visible. Be helpful.

Let's also talk about visibility on social media, because there's gold there too when you use it right. One of my favourite quick-win strategies for content is the STOP Ads. It grabs attention by calling out a behaviour that your audience is currently doing, one that isn't serving them.

Here's a structure you can use:

1. STOP doing [common behaviour your audience is doing]
2. Here's why that's not working.
3. Here's what to do instead.
4. And here's a real example or result.

For example, if I were writing this post for myself, I'd say:

STOP sending emails and waiting for people to reply.

Here's why: Emails can get buried, ignored, or misinterpreted.
Instead, pick up the phone. Start a real conversation.
I did this last month with five previous clients, four rebooked and one referred someone else. The result? A week's worth of revenue in two days.

The human voice builds trust faster than any perfectly written email ever will.

You can adapt this for any industry:

STOP guessing what your clients want. Ask them.
STOP hiding your new offers. Share them clearly.
STOP assuming they'll remember you. Remind them.
This approach works because it's bold, relatable, and solution-driven, and it repositions you as the helpful expert, not the desperate seller.

Ads
One minute, STOP, Before You Spend Another Penny!
I always tell my clients: Don't pour water into a leaky bucket. Ads are powerful, but not when you've neglected your foundation. It's easy to

think more visibility equals more sales. But more often, it just leads to more noise. Instead of chasing strangers with your money, nurture the people who already know you exist. Angela, an online course creator, was frustrated that her Facebook ads were draining her budget with very little return. When we reviewed her business, we found hundreds of people who had signed up for her lead magnets, attended her webinars, and even messaged her with questions but she hadn't followed up. We paused her ad spend and instead focused on a re-engagement sequence titled: "Still dreaming of launching your course?" The emails were conversational, curious, and offered a free clarity call for those still stuck in planning mode.

That re-engagement campaign booked 18 calls and converted 6 into £1,200 course packages a return she never got from her ads.

Moral of the story? Before throwing money at ads, ask yourself: Have I truly nurtured the people who already showed interest in me?

Referrals: Your Clients Know People Who Need You
Referrals don't have to be awkward. In fact, when done with integrity, they're one of the most loving things your clients can do, not just for you, but for the people they refer. They're offering someone in their circle a trusted solution. Let's talk about Jason, a leadership coach who never once asked for a referral, even though his clients raved about him. We introduced a simple but powerful process: at the end of every client engagement, he'd say:

"It's been such an honour to work with you. If there's anyone in your circle who's navigating something similar and could benefit from this kind of support, I'd be grateful for an introduction. I'd also be happy to offer them a free 30-minute clarity call, just as a gift."

He was nervous at first, but within the first month, he received 5 client referrals, 3 of which converted. Why? Because he asked in a way that felt natural, generous, and non-salesy.

Hot tip: Make it easy. Give your clients the words to use. Create a short blurb or link they can share. Offer a gift or discount for referred clients. But most importantly - ask from the heart.

If you've followed along this far, you've already begun to see the incredible power of genuine connection, the kind that doesn't chase sales but attracts them through value, clarity, and care. Whether it's reaching out to existing clients, reactivating old quotes, asking for referrals, or simply showing up with more presence, these strategies aren't just about transactions, they're about transformation. Because every touchpoint is an opportunity to serve. When you stop selling and start serving, the result is deeper trust, more aligned clients, and sustainable success. But connection is only one side of the coin. In the next chapter, we'll go deeper, into the heart of what it truly means to lead in business today. We'll explore how to embody servant leadership, a model where your example becomes your influence, and your service becomes your legacy. You'll learn how to inspire clients not just with what you offer, but with how you show up, with empathy, integrity, and unwavering commitment to their growth.

Let's step into leadership, the kind that transforms lives, builds movements, and sets a new standard for heart-centred success, one where everybody wins.

*Opening my new showroom that
I purposely built in 2007*

marcus elwell
SALES MINDSET TRANSFORMATION

Connect with me on Instagram
for more tips & insights

marcus elwell
SALES MINDSET TRANSFORMATION

CHAPTER SIX

MODELLING SERVANT LEADERSHIP

Inspiring Clients Through Service

A few years ago, a friend of mine, a brilliant wellness coach, told me about a discovery call that changed how she saw sales forever. The client had found her through a referral and booked a free 30-minute session. She showed up flustered and guarded, clearly unsure about whether she wanted to invest in another "program." But instead of trying to impress her with results or rush into her offer, my friend did something powerful. She slowed the moment down. She asked real questions, about the woman's life, her current challenges, what she was truly craving. Not surface-level goals, but the deeper desires. The woman talked. My friend listened. No pressure. Just presence. Just service.

At the end, the woman said, "I don't even know your package details yet, but I already trust you.

"You actually see me."

That client signed up on the spot - not because of a pitch, but because of how she felt: seen, safe, and supported.

That is the heart of servant leadership.

In today's world, people are tired of being sold to. They're overwhelmed by options and noise. What they really want is someone who listens without agenda, who guides with empathy, and who leads with integrity. Someone who serves first, sells second.

In this chapter, it's all about the conversation converter. In this section, we go deeper into the art of authentic sales conversations and explore a proven process I call «Sailing the Seven C›s.» This is more than a technique, it›s a psychology-backed framework for creating genuine, service-led conversations that flow naturally and build trust. Whether you›re on the phone, face-to-face, or even engaging via video calls, this model can be adapted to suit your business and your personal style.

We'll walk through seven key moments that allow you to step into true sales leadership:

Care
Care beyond the sale.

Commitment
Guiding them to take empowered action from a place of clarity.

Convincing
How to build trust and inspire belief without being pushy.

Categories
Categorising the people you are speaking to.

Current
Where they really are right now - practically and emotionally.

Crave
What they truly desire at a soul level.

Consequence
What it's costing them to stay stuck.

This isn't about performance. It's about, you guessed right - connection. This is how we inspire, not pressure. How we serve, not chase. How we lead, not push.

Let's begin with the first moment of servant-led influence: Categories and why recognising what a client feels like (not just what they say) is the foundation of trust.

Categories: The Energetic Starting Point of Service
Before you speak, pitch, or even ask a question - pause.
Because the moment someone enters your world, they're already giving you clues.

- Through their energy.
- Their pace.
- Their posture.
- Their tone.
- Their presence.

And as a servant leader in sales, your first job isn't to prove how brilliant you are. It's to read the room. Feel their frequency.

Tune into their temperament. Discern what kind of support they truly need in that moment. This moment is sacred.

Why?

Because how you respond in the first few minutes determines whether they will trust you – or retreat. Now, this is where something I've emphasised throughout this book comes fully into focus:

Categories aren›t labels to box people in. They are lenses that help you serve them better.

Different buyers need different types of connection.
Some are fast and firm, ready to buy.
Some are thinkers – cautious, calculated, questioning.
Some want to feel seen and safe before they say yes.
Others? Well... some people just aren't your people, and that's okay too. This is why I created a framework called R.I.C.H. It helps you quickly assess the buyer's energetic category so you can align your conversation and posture accordingly.

The R.I.C.H. Buyer Categories

R – Ready
This person has done their homework. They're decisive, direct, and prepared to move forward. You don't need to tiptoe – lead with clarity, and they'll follow. These clients value speed and solutions. So, give it to them straight. Ask for the sale. Close the deal. They're ready – don't slow them down.

I – Inquisitive
These are your curious cats. They're interested but still gathering information. They want to understand the value, the structure, the story behind what you offer. This isn't stalling – it's processing. So slow down, educate, ask good questions, and build the bridge of trust brick by brick.

C – Cautious
Some clients tend to tread lightly. Maybe they've been burned before. Maybe they overthink. Maybe they're terrified of making the wrong move. These people need patience and empathy. Give them space. Answer

their objections before they even ask. And never rush them. The safer they feel, the faster they'll move - on their terms.

H – Hopeless

And finally, there are the ones who... honestly, aren›t in the game. They want everything for nothing. They drain your energy. They talk a lot but take no action. These are not your people. So instead of trying to convince or convert, bless and release. Redirect them kindly - send them to your low-cost resources, your podcast, or your website, then move on.

Why Does This Matter?

Because when you can recognise who's in front of you, you stop selling and start serving. You move from cookie-cutter conversations to custom-fit connection. You save time, energy, and emotional bandwidth. You become magnetic - not just persuasive. And most importantly, you build trust - not through manipulation, but through mutual recognition.

So next time you step into a conversation, whether it's on a sales call, a networking event, or a casual DM...
*   Don't lead with your pitch.
*   Lead with your perception.
*   Use the **R.I.C.H. lens** to guide how you show up.

Because when you categorise with compassion and clarity, you create deeper connection and better conversions - without ever compromising your values.

In the next section, we'll dive into the Current, how to meet clients where they are, not just where you think they should be.

Current: Meet Them Where They Are - Not Where You Think They Should Be

Recognising your client's energetic Category is powerful - it gives you the tone, pace, and posture for how to begin. But once you›ve tuned into who they are, the next step is just as crucial: Uncover where they are right now. Not where you want them to be.

Not where they hope to be. But their actual, raw, present-tense reality. This is where so many entrepreneurs, coaches, and even seasoned sales pros get it wrong. They jump straight into features and benefits... painting a picture of the transformation... before they've even asked:

"Where are you today?"

It's like giving someone directions to the airport - without knowing where they're driving from. No wonder they get lost.

Let's start with this: Curiosity over assumption.

Here are a few essential servant-led questions:
- "What are you currently doing to solve this problem?"
- "What's working for you?"
- "What's not?"
- "What does that actually mean in practical terms?"
- "How long has that been the case?"
- "What results are you seeing from that?"

Don't settle for surface-level responses like, "It's okay," or "Yeah, it's fine." Press gently, lovingly. Not to sell - but to understand.
The goal here is empathy-driven exploration.

You're not prying. You're partnering. You're peeling back the layers to locate the gap between their current reality and their desired result.

Let's look at this Case Study: Sarah, A Wellness Coach
Sarah had a brilliant 90-day transformation program. Dozens of testimonials. Happy clients. But her calls kept ending with, "I'm not ready," or "This feels like a big leap."

When we looked closer, we realised:
She was selling the destination before validating the starting point.
She'd lead with promises of energy, vitality, and full-body transformation. But her prospects were still stuck in the trenches — exhausted, overwhelmed, ashamed, and scared.
So, we made one small but mighty shift.

Every call began with:
"Let's start with where you're at right now — no pressure, no judgment. Just real talk."

That one change opened everything. Her leads felt seen. They felt safe. And most importantly, they felt heard.
Sales stopped feeling like a push. And started feeling like a partnership.
This is what the wrong approach sounds like:
- Talking about what they could have without asking what they're currently facing
- Assuming you know what, they need, before they've even told you
- Using a one-size-fits-all pitch instead of tailored guidance

This is what the servant-led approach sounds like:
- Leading with curiosity, not assumption
- Creating space for their story
- Reflecting their reality with respect and empathy

When you meet someone in their Current, you honour their humanity. You acknowledge their now. You speak into their world, not at it. And that changes everything.
Try this powerful anchor question:
"Can I ask - what does this feel like for you right now, day to day?"

Then... hush.
Hold the space.
Let them pour.

You'll be surprised how often people reveal exactly what they need - if you're quiet long enough to let them.

Because when people feel safe, they open.
When they open, they trust.
And when they trust... they buy.

Pro Tip: The Rapport Deep Dive
This stage is also your golden opportunity to build high-level rapport. Ask questions like:
- "Tell me more about you - how long have you been in business?"
- "What do you love about what you do?"
- "How's life outside of work? Kids? Hobbies?"
- "What gets you up in the morning?"
- "What frustrates you most about where you're at right now?"

People love to talk about themselves. And as they do, they reveal the beliefs, fears, and motivators that drive their decisions. This is your real sales intelligence - not in your script, but in their story.

And here›s the beautiful part:
- As they talk, you listen.
- You lean back.
- You tune in.

Because while they›re unloading, they're also giving you the keys to serve them better - with language, tone, pace, and precision.

And that's how you become unforgettable.

Crave - The Real Desires Beneath the Surface

Once you've connected with someone in their Current, and they feel seen, safe, and heard - something begins to shift. A bridge is built between where they are and where they long to be. And this is where the second part of your servant-led sales conversation begins: Crave.

Now, I don't mean what they say they want on the surface. Many people will tell you what they think they're supposed to want.

"I just want more followers."
"I need to make more sales."
"I want to lose weight."

But these are not the true desires. They're headlines. Soundbites. The socially acceptable answers that don't rock the boat or reveal too much.

Beneath those words are the real cravings:
- The craving for recognition, to feel valued and respected.
- The craving for stability, safety, and peace of mind.
- The craving for confidence, purpose, self-worth, and the feeling that they matter.

Great salespeople - the ones who lead with integrity, with heart, and with service - learn to listen beneath the surface. They don't just hear what's being said. They hear what's trying to be said. And they create a safe space for it to come forward.

Let me share an example.

Nadine, one of my coaching clients, is a brilliant business strategist. She had crafted a powerful high-ticket group program and had plenty of discovery calls lined up. Her calendar looked healthy, but the conversions weren't. People were showing interest but not committing. Something wasn't landing. When we reviewed a few of her conversations, the pattern became clear. Nadine was doing a good job of connecting with where the client was currently struggling. She was reflecting their pain with empathy and validation. But she was stopping there. She wasn't moving them into possibility. She wasn't inviting them to dream. She wasn't asking them what they craved.

So, we made a shift. A simple, powerful addition to her sales script:

"If everything were working perfectly six months from now, what would life and business look and feel like for you?"

That one question changed the entire energy of her conversations. Instead of staying stuck in their logical, analytical mind, clients dropped into emotion. Into vision. Into desire. They opened up. They shared more. And from that place of emotional truth, her program wasn't just another solution. It became the clear next step.

This is what the Crave stage is all about.

It's your opportunity to ask deeper questions that move your prospect out of logic and into feeling. From the head to the heart. From "How much is it?" to "How would this change everything?"

When you're in this stage of the conversation, you might say something like:

"You've just told me where things are right now, and I really appreciate your honesty. Let's shift gears for a moment. Let's imagine I waved a magic wand... What does amazing look like for you?
In life? In business?"

Let them speak.

Then follow up with the goldmine question:

"And why is that important to you?"

Push past the first answer. The first one is often polite or rehearsed.
"I want to travel more."

Okay, why?
"I want freedom."

Why?

"Because I want to spend more time with my kids. I missed so much of their childhood already..."

There it is!

That's the real stuff. The emotional stuff. That's what drives action. When you stay with them long enough to uncover what they truly crave, not only do you gain clarity as the guide - but you also earn trust as a partner. They now know you're not just trying to sell them something. You're helping them walk toward something that matters. And this is important: cravings are deeply emotional. They are rooted in identity. In healing. In meaning. In self-permission. The role of a servant-hearted salesperson isn't to impose a dream. It's to awaken it.

Most people don't lack desire - they lack space to voice it.

Your role is to ask the questions that draw it out.

"Why now?"
"Why haven't you done this before?"
"What's different this time?"

These questions are not interrogations. They are invitations. And when your prospect answers them honestly, something profound happens - they begin to believe in the possibility again.

That belief creates momentum. And momentum creates movement.

Here's what most entrepreneurs get wrong at this stage:
- They sell features, not feelings.
- They talk about what their product does, instead of what it means.
- They assume the client is making a rational decision, when in reality, most decisions are emotional - and only justified logically later.

Here's what servant leaders do instead:
- They listen for the longing.
- They reflect the deeper desire back in the client's own words.
- They hold the vision without rushing the sale.
- They make the conversation about the client's transformation, not their own transaction.

And this is key: you must earn the right to move the conversation forward.

You do that by asking, not pitching.
By leaning back, not pushing forward.
By holding space, not filling silence.

Every stage of this process matters. If you skip this one - if you move too quickly into the close - you miss the moment of emotional connection that creates commitment.

So slow down. Ask big questions. Stay curious.

Because when you meet someone in their Crave - and reflect that craving back to them with sincerity and service - you create a connection that makes selling unnecessary.

They don't feel sold to.
They feel supported.
They feel seen.
They feel ready.
And that's where the real work begins.

Consequences - Serving Clients by Reflecting the Cost of Inaction

Once you've helped your client unpack their Current and tap into their Crave, the next natural progression is not to sell, but to serve them by holding space for the truth.

What truth?
If nothing changes... nothing changes.
It's time to gently explore Consequences.
Not to create fear.
Not to push.
Not to manipulate.
But to lovingly reflect the reality of inaction.

Because here's what I've learned repeatedly in sales, leadership, and life:
Most people aren't stuck because they don't know what to do.
They're stuck because they haven't fully faced what it's costing them to stay where they are.

It's more comfortable for many to tolerate a known discomfort than to face the uncertainty of transformation.
They know they're overwhelmed.
They know they've outgrown their current habits or mindset.
They know there's more available - but stepping into the unknown feels risky.

So, they stall.

They sit.

They say, "Maybe later."

And this, right here, is where most well-meaning entrepreneurs fumble the moment.

They try to "pep talk" their prospect back into momentum with statements like:

"But imagine how good it will feel when you're earning more!"
"You'll feel so empowered when you take this step!"

Yes, inspiration has a place.
But without clarity on what's at stake, inspiration can feel like fantasy.

Let me tell you about Adam.

Adam is a brilliant business coach I mentored. He was a heart-led, visionary type - always rooting for his clients, always painting the big picture of possibility. But when his leads hesitated, he'd go straight into high-energy motivation.

The problem?

His clients weren't ready to leap forward because they hadn't fully grasped what it was costing them to stay where they were.
So, we reframed his approach. Instead of rushing to possibility, he slowed down. He started saying:

"Totally understand. Can I ask something gently?
If nothing changes over the next 3 or 6 months, what will that cost you -
emotionally, financially, energetically?"

That one shift opened everything.
His clients paused. Reflected.
They saw clearly, some for the first time, that staying stuck wasn't neutral - it was costing them something precious: time, confidence, income, peace of mind.
They didn't feel pushed.
They felt seen.

And they started moving forward - not because Adam pressured them, but because he created a space of honesty, reflection, and alignment. That's what servant-hearted consequence is all about.

You're not the hero swooping in with a fix.

You're the guide holding up a mirror and saying, "Let's look at what happens if you don't move forward. Gently. Honestly. Together."

Try asking questions like:

- "So, let's say nothing changes. Where does that leave you in 6 months?"
- "What does that mean for your business? Your peace of mind? Your energy?"
- "Can you continue to carry on like this? Is that sustainable?"
- "What impact is this already having on your relationships, your finances, your confidence?"

Let them tell you the truth.
Let them feel the weight of staying stuck - not to create pressure, but to create perspective.

And if they start to brush it off with a "Yeah, I guess I'll be okay," gently bring them back:

"Earlier, you shared that having more time freedom was important to you. If things stay the same, what does that mean for that goal? What would you have to sacrifice or postpone?"

This is where you reconnect their words to their reality.
You don't need to tell them what they'll lose.
Let them walk themselves there.

You can even go a layer deeper.
"Out of curiosity... what beliefs would need to shift for you to move forward?"

"What story are you still telling yourself that might be keeping you stuck?"

"Be honest - are you just talking a good game? Or are you ready to do something different?"

Now, that last one is bold.
But if asked with care and compassion, it's powerful.
It invites your client to call themselves forward.
It helps them self-identify as someone who acts rather than someone who talks about action.
And once they've done that?
They've already begun to move.

Because here's the truth:

Sometimes it's not the promise of the dream that moves people forward.
It's the reality of the cost of delay.
And when you can guide someone to face that without guilt or shame,
you become more than a salesperson.
You become a partner in their breakthrough.
They don't feel cornered.
They feel clear.
They feel respected.
They feel ready.
And you've earned the right - not to close a deal—but to continue a
conversation that may just change their life.

Next up is Convince, and spoiler alert: it's not what you think.
Servant leaders don't "convince" in the traditional sense. Instead, they
build trust through transparency, proof, and alignment.

Great, let's move into the next section:

Convince — Building Trust Through Truth, Not Tactics
By now, you've walked your potential client through a deep, meaningful
journey. You've helped them recognise where they are (Current),
connect with what they long for (Crave), and reflect on the cost of
inaction (Consequences). Now you arrive at the moment many people
dread: "the close."
But let's be honest...
This isn't the time to flip into "persuasion mode." This isn't about high-
pressure tactics or overcoming objections with clever rebuttals.
Because if you've truly served them through the process, this moment
isn't about getting the sale - it's about earning it.

Here's the heart of this phase:
Convincing isn't about coercing. It's about clarifying.
It's about empowering your potential client to say yes with peace, not
pressure.

You've listened deeply. Now you lead clearly.
Let's say you're a mindset coach for entrepreneurs. You've just had
a powerful conversation with a woman named Lisa. She's burnt out,
overwhelmed, and craving clarity. She's resonated with everything
you've shared, but now she says:

"I really want this... but I've tried so many things before that didn't work."

Now here's where most people mess it up.

They start scrambling, saying things like:

"Oh no, trust me, this is different!"
"I promise, this time will work!"

That's not reassuring. That's desperate.

As a servant-hearted leader, your response sounds more like:

"That makes perfect sense. Would it be helpful if I shared a couple of real stories of people just like you who felt the same way—and what happened for them once they started?" That's how you build trust.

Not by promising.
Not by pushing.

But by aligning.
By proving.

By serving their decision-making process.
Sell through stories, not scripts.
This is where your case studies, testimonials, and client transformations come in - not to brag, but to build belief.
If you haven't got a catalogue of past clients yet, use your own story. Or stories from people you've helped in informal ways - friends, colleagues, or even yourself - framed as examples.

Paint the picture:
•   Show what life looked like before the decision.
•   Describe the shift that happened after they said yes.
•   Be specific. Be relatable. Be real.

Here›s what you›re doing in this phase:
•   You're making the invisible benefits visible.
•   You're connecting the dots between where they are and how your offer bridges the gap.
•   You're positioning your solution, not pushing it.

Your job here is to communicate value clearly and calmly.

"Here's how the program works.
Here's what you get.
Here's how we support you.

Here's what's included.
Here's how we've helped others in the same situation.
And here's why I believe it can work for you too."

And yes – this is also the moment to talk about the investment.
Don't shy away from the money.
Say it with confidence and kindness:

"Let's walk through the investment. Most of my clients pay in full, but we also have a payment plan. What feels best for you?"

"Would you prefer to pay via credit card, debit card, or would you like a secure payment link?"

Speak about money like it's normal – because it is. This is a business conversation. You've earned the right to make the invitation, and now they need clarity around logistics, not anxiety around pressure.

Handle hesitation with heart

If they need to speak to a partner or pause to reflect, don't get defensive. Instead, guide them with grace.

"That makes total sense. I want you to feel confident about your decision. Would it help to recap what's included and what outcomes we're focused on so you can have that conversation with clarity?"
Or...

"Can I ask – what would help you feel certain that this is the right next step for you?"

This is not about getting the yes at all costs.
It's about making sure that the yes is whole, rooted, and honest.
Because when people feel safe, seen, and supported...
They say yes with joy, not fear.

The Servant-Hearted Close Is Simple
"Based on everything you've shared, I believe this is a great fit. Do you feel the same?"

[Wait for their answer. Listen deeply.]

"Beautiful. So, the next step is..."

At this point, walk them through the payment process confidently. Be clear, warm, and professional.

- Let them know exactly what happens next.
- Lay out the expectations.
- Reassure them of your support.

You're not *closing* them.
You're *welcoming* them.

This Is How You Convince - with Care, Clarity, and Confidence
Because real convincing is never manipulative.
It's not loud or flashy.
It's not gimmicky or slick.
It's grounded.
It's truthful.
It's rooted in service.
And when done right, it doesn't feel like "convincing" at all.
It feels like a sacred agreement.
One that transforms not just a business deal - but a life.

Excellent! Let's move into the final piece of this framework, the moment of decision, action, and responsibility:

Commit: Leading Clients into Empowered Action

If you've made it this far with your client - congratulations. You've done what many never do.
You've led with service, not ego.
You've facilitated connection, not control.
You've helped them recognise their Category, get honest about their Current, dream into what they Crave, voice their Concerns, reflect on the Consequences, and find confidence through Convince.
And now, you arrive at the final "C" in this servant-hearted sales framework: Commit.

This is the moment they say "yes." Or at least, they want to.
But here's the truth: Commitment is emotional.
It requires trust. It demands vulnerability. It asks the client to go from intention to investment—putting their time, money, and energy behind the vision they just dared to speak aloud.

Your role now?

Not to push.

Not to beg.
Not to shrink.

Your role is to stand beside them - not behind, not ahead - and lead them gently but clearly across the threshold of decision.

Why Most Entrepreneurs Fumble the Close

Many well-meaning entrepreneurs either:
Rush this part,
Avoid it out of fear of sounding too "salesy," or
Assume the decision is already made and go quiet.

But the servant-hearted entrepreneur stays present.
You've earned the right to guide them forward, so don't abandon the process now.

Don't whisper when it's time to lead.
Let's look at a simple way to do that:

"Based on everything you've shared, I really believe this is a strong fit for you. Do you feel the same?"

[Wait for their response. Let them affirm it.]

"Beautiful. So, here's how we get started..."

From here, lead with **clarity** and **calm authority:**
• Share the next steps.
• Outline how the onboarding works.
• Explain what they'll receive, when, and how.
• Let them know what to expect from you—and what you'll need from them.

When you do this well, commitment becomes safe. Tangible. Empowering.

Talk About the Investment Like a Leader
Let's not dance around it—money matters.
Don't flinch when it's time to discuss payment. That hesitation creates insecurity for your client. Instead, speak with grounded confidence and options:

"Most clients pay in full, but we also offer a split-pay option. What works best for you - credit card, debit, or would you prefer a secure link?"

Or:

"To get started, I'll just need your payment details. I'll walk you through everything."

This is where you lean into their buyer type. If they're cautious, slow down. Offer reassurance. If they're decisive, keep it sharp and direct. Match their energy while maintaining your calm presence.
And remember - people will mirror your certainty. So, if you believe in the transformation you're offering, don't just sell it... stand on it.

Anticipate Concerns - Don't Avoid Them!

We will touch on this in a bit when I speak about the salt that you need to sprinkle all throughout the conversation or what I call the silent C

Let's go now to the final C in the system, and it is a very crucial one to remember

Care – Care Beyond the Sale

The first thing to take note of and remember, is that care Doesn't Stop at Commitment There's a moment in every client journey that most entrepreneurs completely underestimate. It's the moment right after someone says yes.

Not the sales page.
Not the pitch.
Not the discovery call.
Not even the commitment.

It's the quiet moment after the sale - when the adrenaline wears off and doubt creeps in.

This is the moment where trust is either confirmed... or questioned. Why?

Because the world has trained people to expect disappointment. They›ve been sold to before. They›ve been promised before. They've said yes, only to be let down - again.

So now, even when they say yes to you, a tiny voice still whispers:

"Was this the right choice?"
"What if this is like last time?"
"Did I just waste my money… again?"

They don't ask it out loud.
They smile and nod.
But inwardly, they retreat into Google searches, old reviews, or even back to scrolling – mentally hedging their bets.
And this is where servant-hearted entrepreneurs separate themselves from the rest.
Because while others breathe a sigh of relief after the payment comes through, you step in.
You step up.
You serve harder.
Because you understand something most people miss:
Care doesn't end at the sale.
Care begins at the sale.

The First 20 Minutes Matter More Than You Think

Let's get practical.
Within 20 minutes of someone committing - send a message.
Not a templated "Thanks for your payment" email.
A message.
One that feels warm, intentional, and personal. Something that says:
"I see you. I honour this decision. I'm here for you."
That could be a voice note.
A video.
A personalised email.
Even a quick Loom screen recording walking them through what happens next.
It doesn't have to be long. It just has to be real.
You're not just providing a service. You're confirming their faith in you.

Give Them Certainty. Give Them Direction.

Care is not just about emotion. It's about structure.
After someone buys, they want to know:
• What happens next?
• What do I need to do?
• What should I expect?
• Who do I contact if I get stuck?

They don't want to guess.
They want to feel safe.
So, give them certainty. Lay out the path ahead.
Whether that means delivering a welcome pack, sending login details, booking a kick-off call, or giving them pre-work, the goal is the same:

Remove confusion. Build momentum.
Because here's the truth:
CONFUSION is the enemy of commitment whilst CLARITY is the soil trust grows in.

Invite Them into More Than a Program - Invite Them into a Mission
What if we stopped thinking of sales as transactions, and started thinking of them as initiations?
When someone chooses to work with you, they're not just buying a coaching package or a workshop.

They're saying:
"I want to become someone different."
"I believe change is possible."
"I'm ready to take a step."

That is sacred.
So, treat it that way.
Show them they haven't just purchased something - they've partnered with someone.

Remind them of what they're stepping into. A mission. A message. A movement.
"This isn't just about building a business - this is about building a legacy."
"This isn't just about wellness — it's about freedom in your body and your life."
"This isn't just about income — it's about becoming who you were made to be."
That's what care sounds like.
That's what deepens buy-in.

The Close Is Not the End — It's the Beginning
We often call it a "sales close," but if we're honest, it's not a close at all.
It's an opening.
It's the beginning of transformation.
It's the moment someone stops dreaming about change... and starts walking into it.
So don't disappear after the sale. Don't treat the end of the transaction

as the end of the relationship.
If anything, it's where your leadership matters most.
Follow up.
Check in.
Celebrate wins.
Respond with compassion.
Remind them why they started.
Because when someone commits to you, they don't just want a product.
They want presence.

Build an Onboarding Experience That Surprises Them

Here's where you get to be strategic and soulful:
- Send a branded welcome pack with all key information.
- Deliver a short video or note celebrating their commitment.
- Let them know exactly what happens next (dates, calls, tasks).
- Share testimonials or case studies they haven't seen yet — stories that reflect their own journey.

This builds anticipation, not anxiety.
It tells them, *"You made a wise decision. You're in good hands."*

From Client to Advocate - The Ripple Effect of Care
Let me say it plainly:
When you show up after the sale, people stick around.
They stay longer.
They go deeper.
They refer more.
Because your care becomes their confidence.
They don't just remember what you sold them - they remember how you made them feel.
That's the difference between a client and a lifetime advocate.
Final Thought: Love Them Loud
The best way to stand out in a saturated market?

Follow through when others fall off.
So many people go quiet once they've got the money. They think their job is done.
But not you.
You're not just collecting payments.
You're collecting people.
You're building partnerships.
You're stewarding transformations.
So, show them what that looks like.

- Be consistent.
- Be available.
- Be human.

True service doesn't end with a sale - and it certainly doesn't disappear when there isn't one. One of the greatest marks of a servant-hearted entrepreneur is how they show up for the people who don't say yes.

Not everyone will be ready to buy. That's reality. But no one should ever feel dropped, ignored, or dismissed simply because they didn't commit. People remember how you made them feel, and sometimes, the seeds of future relationships are planted in how you handle a "not now."

That's why I encourage you to follow up no more than 20 minutes after your call - regardless of outcome. It could be a voice note, a short video, or even a quick email like:

"Just reaching out to say it was great to connect with you. I really appreciated our conversation. As mentioned, I'll give you a call next week, but in the meantime, if anything comes up, I'm here."

Or, if they have decided to move forward:

"Thank you for saying yes! I'm genuinely excited to work with you and walk with you toward your goals. You've made a powerful decision, and I'm here for you every step of the way."

If you're sending a video – something I highly recommend and is my main go to – it would be something like:

"Hey there! I just wanted to send you this quick video so you can see who you've been speaking with. My name's [Your Name]—this is me, a real human behind the screen."

In a world full of AI and perfectly polished posts, it's easy to forget there's a real person on the other side. For me, it's all about trust, connection, and building real rapport. So here I am - just showing up as I am, and you should do the same too.

Whether they committed or not, the goal is the same: connection, reassurance, and consistency.

Buyer's remorse often creeps in during silence and before you know it they are wondering if they have made a mistake, did they go with the right person or investment, then they start to scroll again on search for the 'right person' and you know how the algorithms are before you know it someone else in your industry has showed up which then means that there is a cancellation call or email about to be sent to you. Your job at this point is to stop them from scrolling, to make them feel at peace with their investment or if they have not yet committed to have you so much at the forefront of their minds that when they are ready there's no doubt that you are the right one to get them from point A to Point B. When those that have committed don't hear from you, fear fills the gap. But when you reach out with warmth, integrity, and a spirit of service, you disarm that fear. You stay in their world. And even if today wasn't the day they bought, you've made a lasting impression - and built a bridge they'll be more likely to cross when the time is right.

Because the real win isn't just the sale - it's the relationship.

So, let them feel your commitment every step of the way - not just at the sale, but through every step after it.

Because when care becomes your culture, your clients become your community. And that's what real impact is made of, and this is what CARE beyond the sale is all about.

So now that we have completed all the C's lets proceed by speaking about a different C. Earlier, I mentioned the salt that you should be sprinkling throughout the conversation – The silent C. here I am speaking about Concerns, you would have seen it mentioned a few times throughout.

Concerns: Navigating Fear with Empathy and Leadership

You must Anticipate Concerns - Don't Avoid Them!

Throughout the entire journey, you should've been checking in - acknowledging unspoken objections and naming the elephants in the room. Don't wait until now to handle all their resistance.

That's too late.

Instead, address it naturally:

"A lot of people I speak to feel hesitant at this point - especially if they've tried things that didn't work before. You mentioned earlier that you had a similar experience. Can I share how this is different?"

Use stories, case studies, and examples to affirm their fear without amplifying it.

Handle concerns before they become roadblocks.

After your client dares to express what they truly crave, something else almost always follows: Concern.
It's the pause after the dream.
The hesitation after the hope.
The "what if" after the "I want."

Even when clients feel excited about the possibility of working with you or taking the next step, fear will often creep in, sometimes loudly, sometimes subtly. And that's okay, because fear is part of the transformation process. What matters most is how you respond to those concerns.

Let's revisit Nadine, the strategist I spoke about earlier. After she learned to help clients name their craving, she noticed something: as soon as they voiced their vision, they also started listing all the reasons it might not happen.
- "What if I fail again?"
- "I've tried other programs and nothing worked."
- "It's a big investment... what if I can't make it back?"
- "I'm not sure I have the time right now."

And here's where many entrepreneurs make a critical mistake:
They get defensive.
They try to convince.
They bypass the fear and press harder on the pitch.
But servant leaders do the opposite.
They slow down.
They listen. They empathise. They validate. And most importantly, they lead with service, not pressure.

Here's what that looks like in practice:
When a client says, "I'm worried this won't work for me,"
You say, *"I completely understand. Trying something new can feel risky, especially when you've been let down before. Can I ask what specifically feels uncertain for you?"*

Now, instead of ignoring the concern, you're inviting dialogue. You're showing that their safety and clarity matter more than the sale.

You're modelling leadership that builds trust.

Because the truth is, every big decision carry risks, but when someone feels seen, heard, and supported, they're more likely to move forward with confidence.

Let me be clear: concerns are not objections to be "overcome."

They are emotional roadblocks that require connection and clarity.
So instead of resisting them, welcome concerns as part of the process.
This is where you get to lead, not with persuasion, but with compassion, and when you lead someone through their concern, you not only earn their business...

You earn their trust.

So, let's recap the full model you've just walked through:

Care
Care beyond
the sale

Commit
Lead them into
empowered
action with
confidence

Convince
Build trust
through clarity,
not pressure.

Categories
Understand who
you're talking to.

Current
Discover where
they are now.

Crave
Uncover what
they deeply
want.

Consequence
Gently reflect what staying
stuck is costing them.

The Hidden Engine Behind the Seven Cs: Uncovering the Belief That's Been Blocking the Breakthrough

At the core of this entire process - the Seven Cs of Servant-Hearted Sales - lies one ultimate goal: 'Getting under the hood,' I mentioned this briefly earlier.

Uncovering and shifting the belief that's been holding your client back.

Not manipulate.
Not convince by force.
But uncover truth - and then serve them through it.

Because here's what you must understand:

Sales is never really about price, or time, or the "right strategy." It's always about belief.

Somewhere beneath the surface of every "no," every "maybe," every "I'll think about it," is a story they've been telling themselves:
"I'm not ready."
"I've failed before."
"My partner wouldn't support this."
"What if I lose money again?"
"I've always been like this..."
Your job is not to slap positivity over that.
Your job is to get under the hood.
And every step of this process - Category, Current, Crave, Concern, Consequence, Convince, Commit - gives you a different tool to dig just a little deeper.

From Surface to Soul, You're Digging for the Belief Beneath the Block

Let's break this down.
In the Current phase, you're not just gathering information. You're listening for patterns - habits, choices, coping mechanisms.
Ask enough of the right questions, and eventually, they'll say something like:
"I guess I've just always played it safe..."
"I've tried before, and it didn't work out."
"I'm not sure I'm the kind of person who could..."
There it is - the belief.
Right there, quietly driving their reality like a backseat driver with a megaphone.

In the Crave phase, you help them voice their desire - but you don't stop there. You ask:

- *Why is that important to you?*
- *Why now?*
- *How would that change your life?*
- *And how would that make you feel?*
-

Because here's a universal truth:
If they can't feel it, they can't believe it. And if they can't believe it, they won't commit.

That's why emotional resonance matters. When you help them emotionally experience the freedom, abundance, ease, or confidence they're craving - even just for a moment - you begin to break the grip of the old belief.

Tie the Thread - Bring It Full Circle

When you arrive at the Consequence stage, you gently reflect:

"So, what happens if nothing changes?"
"What does life look like if you're still in the same place 3, 6, 12 months from now?"

Then - here's where the masterful shift happens - you tie it back:

"Earlier, you told me the reason you haven't taken action until now is because deep down, you didn't think you were good enough / ready / allowed / supported. If that belief doesn't change…, do you really think the outcome will?"

You're not confronting them.
You're inviting them.
You're becoming the guide that holds up the mirror with compassion and says:

"What story would you need to believe instead - to actually move forward?"

Let them answer it.
Let them say it in their own words.
Let them own it.
That's when the real sales transformation happens - not because you pushed them…
But because you walked with them through their own story and helped them rewrite the ending.

This is why emotional state matters.
We don't buy from logic.
We don't act from information alone.
We act from emotion.
From desire.
From belief.
From vision.

So, when they're in that emotional state - when they can feel the life they crave, and the cost of staying where they are - that's when commitment becomes possible.

Not because they were sold.

Because they were seen.
Because they were served.
Because they were given a safe space to shift their belief.

The Role of the Servant-Seller

Let me be clear:
You are not a hype-man.
You are not a fixer.
You are not the hero of their story.
You are the mirror, the mentor, and the midwife of a belief shift.
Your role is to lovingly challenge the lie.
To elevate the truth.
To show them they can become who they were designed to be.
And when you do that, every sale becomes a sacred exchange.

This is how you sell from service. Not pressure. Not manipulation. Just deep connection, honest conversation, belief shift and alignment. Because here's the thing, when sales feel this natural; you stop fearing them. You start enjoying them. And you become magnetic. This is the power of modelling servant leadership. It's not about charm or perfect words. It's about presence, empathy, and deep integrity. Because when you lead with love, clarity, and service, everybody wins.

In the next chapter, we'll explore how to magnetise success by attracting opportunities through genuine service around this heart-led approach, so that serving doesn't burn you out, and you can create sustainable success by scaling service, not stress.

With my friends & great support throughout my journey Jas, Paul & Jason doing the hyrox with me

CHAPTER SEVEN

MAGNETISING SUCCESS

Attracting Opportunities Through Genuine Service

Have you ever watched a campfire fade? It doesn't happen all at once. The blaze that once roared with life dims slowly, flickering into embers before disappearing into ash. What keeps the fire alive isn't just the wood, it's the care. The attention. The willingness to tend it, poke at it, feed it, nurture it. Without that, even the strongest flame will die out. Business, much like that fire, isn't just sparked by an idea, a sale, or a moment of connection. It's kept alive by how you nurture the relationships you ignite along the way. The truth is anyone can make a sale. But what happens after? That's where the magic lies. This chapter is about keeping that fire alive, not through manipulation or pressure, but through genuine, consistent service that transforms transactions into trust, and customers into community. Just as a seasoned camper tends their flame with intention, the most successful entrepreneurs build their reputations by tending to people, consistently, sincerely, and with heart.

Let's explore what it really takes to become magnetic in your business, where success isn't just pursued, but attracted by the way you serve. Have you ever experienced that moment after buying something, maybe a service, a product, or a course, when the initial excitement wears off and you›re left wondering, "Was this really worth it?" Maybe no one followed up with you, no one checked in to see how you were doing, and the connection that was built during the sales process suddenly disappeared. That feeling of being forgotten is a universal experience, and it›s one that every entrepreneur, business owner, and sales professional must actively work to avoid creating for their clients.

This final chapter is so important because many people think the job is done once the sale is closed. But in truth, that's where the real work begins. The way you nurture, serve, and support your client's post-sale determines whether you create a legacy brand or simply make a quick buck. Because how you do anything is how you do everything. We've all heard the sobering statistics: a high percentage of businesses fail within the first year and even more don't make it to year three. Why? Because they focus so heavily on acquisition that they forget about retention. They chase new leads and fresh opportunities while neglecting the goldmine they already have, the clients who've already said "yes."

That's why this chapter is about more than just customer service, it's about **C.A.R.E.S.** an acronym to guide you in how to Continue the Journey with your clients and magnetise lifelong opportunities through genuine service. This isn't about scripts or surface-level engagement. It's about being real. It's about being the kind of business that people talk about at dinner parties, the kind of person who over-delivers, surprises, delights, and remembers the small details. How do you keep showing the love? Check in, even when you don't have to. Celebrate milestones.

Offer value without asking for anything in return. When you launch a new deal, don't forget your existing clients, offer them something extra, something exclusive. Because when you show people that they matter after the sale, they stay, they talk, and they bring others with them.

In today's digital world, where automation and A.I can handle the logistics, there's no excuse not to remain deeply human. Use technology to support the relationship, not replace it. Schedule personal check-ins, send voice notes, remember birthdays, send a bottle of wine or a thank-you card. Do the things most won't.

Because those small, thoughtful gestures create waves. They build trust. They deepen relationships. They turn customers into your greatest sales force, people who not only stay with you but tell everyone they know about you. And the best part? They've already paid you to do it. They're paying clients who become your raving fans. That's the power of showing the love.

So, as we enter this final phase of the book, I want you to lean in. Yes, we're at the end, but this is the beginning of your next level. Because when you embrace service as your superpower, when you CARE deeply and consistently, success stops being a struggle. It becomes magnetised.

Let's explore exactly how to do that. Let's turn clients into lifers, service into impact, and care into currency.

Let's show them the love

Great! Let's begin with the first part of the C.A.R.E.S. framework: Continue the Journey.

Many entrepreneurs believe the sale is the destination. But in heart-centred service, the sale is simply the starting point of a much more meaningful journey - a journey of transformation, trust, and true connection. Think about the last time you bought something that genuinely changed your life. Maybe it was a coaching program, a wellness retreat, or a product that solved a nagging problem. What made it unforgettable wasn't just the solution, it was how you were treated after you said "yes." The welcome you received, the support you felt, the consistent check-ins, the extra value that made you feel like more than just a number. That's what «continuing the journey» looks like, and it's the difference between a single transaction and a loyal, lifelong client.

Far too often, business owners treat the sale like the finish line, quickly **153** moving on to the next lead, the next conversion, the next chase. But here's the truth: your greatest opportunities for impact, referrals, and recurring revenue lie in how you show up after the sale. This is your moment to solidify trust, deliver transformation, and magnetise long-term success. It doesn't take grand gestures. Sometimes, it's as simple as a welcome video, a follow-up email that asks, *"How are you getting on?"* or a handwritten thank you card. Sometimes it's showing up in their inbox with a resource they didn't even know they needed. Other times, it's hopping on a call just to see how they're progressing, not to pitch, but to care.

In a world that's automated and transactional, continuing the journey is what makes you unforgettable. It's what makes people say, "They didn't just sell to me, they saw me, heard me, helped me." That's how you become the go-to, the trusted brand, the one they can't wait to recommend.
Next, let's explore a skill that makes this ongoing journey even more powerful: Active Listening.

If continuing the journey is the vehicle, active listening is the fuel that keeps it moving forward with power and purpose. Most people listen to reply. Heart-centred entrepreneurs listen to understand. And that one shift in intention changes everything. Active listening is more than hearing words, it's about being fully present. It's tuning into what your client is really saying, reading between the lines, noticing tone, pace, body language (if you're face-to-face or on video), and even the silence between their sentences. In that space, people reveal their hopes, fears, and desires, often without even realising it. Here's what many entrepreneurs get wrong: they listen just enough to identify a pain point and immediately jump in with a solution. But when you interrupt the story, you interrupt the trust. You miss out on the deeper truth your client is trying to express. You miss the opportunity to make them feel safe, seen, and significant.

A business coach once told me she had a client who'd signed up for her premium program but had gone quiet just two weeks in. Instead of sending a templated "Just checking in" message, she picked up the phone and said, "I just want to understand how you're feeling right now, no pitch, no pressure." That simple act of presence opened the floodgates. The client admitted she was feeling overwhelmed, unsure if she belonged in the group. With that truth on the table, the coach was able to respond with care, adjust the support offered, and keep the transformation alive. That client stayed, referred two more, and later upgraded her package.

That's the power of active listening. It's the difference between a sale that slips away and a relationship that deepens.

So how can you become a better listener?

- **Put away distractions.** Close the tabs, silence the phone, turn off notifications.
- **Repeat back what you hear.** Use phrases like, "What I'm hearing is..." or "It sounds like you're saying..."
- **Ask deeper questions.** "Tell me more about that," or "What does that mean for you?"
- **Hold space.** Sometimes people just need a pause to find their words. Don't rush to fill it.

Remember: when people feel heard, they lean in. They open up. They trust. And trust is the true currency of any long-lasting business.
Up next, we'll talk about how to keep that trust strong even when things don't go perfectly, with a powerful habit called Resolving Issues Quickly.

Shall we keep going?

Great! Let's move on to the next part of the C.A.R.E.S. framework:

Resolve Issues Quickly

No matter how excellent your product or service is, issues will arise. Deliveries get delayed. Expectations get miscommunicated. Life throws curveballs. And when those moments come, your response becomes your reputation. Too many entrepreneurs and business owners fall into the trap of silence when something goes wrong. They hope the problem goes unnoticed. They avoid the difficult conversation. They wait, stall, or worse, blame the client.
But here's the truth: It's not the mistake that breaks trust; it's how you handle it.

Think about the last time you had a bad experience as a customer. Maybe a delivery didn't arrive on time, or a coach didn't follow up when they promised. What made the experience worse? The mistake, or the fact that nobody acknowledged it.

Now flip the script. Imagine a brand or business that made a mistake, but they owned it immediately. They reached out without you needing to chase. They apologised sincerely, fixed it swiftly, maybe even offered a little extra as a gesture of goodwill. How did that make you feel? **155**

Relieved. Respected. Loyal.

When you resolve issues quickly, you transform a potential loss into a lasting connection. You show your clients that their experience matters more to you than your ego. That your word isn't just a selling point, it's a standard.

Here's how to put that into practice:

- **Respond fast.** Don't let issues fester. Even if you don't have a full answer yet, acknowledge the concern.
- **Take ownership.** Even if it wasn't your fault, take responsibility for finding the solution.
- **Communicate clearly.** Be transparent about what happened, what you're doing about it, and when they can expect resolution.
- **Go one step further.** A small gesture, like a bonus resource, a discount, or simply a heartfelt thank you, can turn frustration into admiration.

One of the fastest ways to lose a client is to ignore a concern. One of the fastest ways to gain a raving fan is to solve it with grace and speed.

So, remember issues aren't the enemy. Indifference is.

Let's keep going, because the next piece is where the magic really starts to multiply: 'Exceed Expectations by Under-Promising and Over-Delivering.' Well, I should say, that's what people say, and I will tell you what I think about that in a minute.

Perfect! Let's move into the next section of the C.A.R.E.S. framework:

Exceed Expectations by Delivering What You Promised - and Then Some

Let's clear the air on a common phrase in business:

"Under-promise and over-deliver."

Sounds clever, right? Like a sneaky magician's trick - set the bar low, then shock them with a rabbit out of a hat.

But here's the truth: I've never liked it. And if you're building a service-led, values-based business rooted in integrity, you shouldn't like it either.

Why?

Because in this heart-centred world of entrepreneurship, it's not about under-promising - it's about transparent promising and wholehearted delivering.
You don't need smoke and mirrors.
You don't need to hold back to create surprise.
What you need is this:
Say what you're going to do.
Do what you said you'd do.
And then show up with everything you›ve got.
That's where the magic is.

Say It on the Tin - And Mean It

One of my key selling points - one I teach my clients to own without flinching - is this:

"Whatever I put on the tin, I deliver. Fully. Faithfully. No fluff. No excuses."

People don't need vague promises wrapped in mystery.
They need certainty.
That means being 100% clear about what's included in your offer.
Spell it out.
Price it accordingly.
Put value on it without apology.
And once they say yes?

Deliver every ounce of it as if it was your name, your character, your legacy on the line — because it is.

But then... Go Even Further

Not through deceptive under-promising.
But through purposeful, generous follow-through.
It's the difference between doing what's expected, and doing what's transformational.
You're not trying to wow with gimmicks.
You're showing your client what it feels like to be fully served.

That could look like:
- A personal video message welcoming them to your program.
- A resource or bonus you didn't list in the original offer, but you know will help them.
- Giving a bit more time or attention during a tough week.
- Anticipating a need before they say it.

- Following up just when they're about to give up.

These aren't surprises. They're reflections of your standard.

Own Your Price - Then Deliver on It Like Your Reputation Depends on It

Many business owners crumble the moment they're challenged on price.

They fumble.
They shrink.
They start slashing numbers or throwing in bonuses just to "sweeten the deal."

Let's flip the script.

When someone questions your rate, meet them with clarity and confidence:

"Yes, I may not be the cheapest, and I'm not trying to be. Here's why I charge what I charge: I've stripped away guesswork. I've factored in the time, tools, strategy, and experience that gets you the result. What I deliver is airtight — and my clients pay for peace of mind, not patchwork pricing."

You're not in the discount business.
You're in the transformation business.
And when someone invests, they're not just buying your time - they're buying your **certainty,** your **structure,** and your **track record.**

Don›t Just Meet Standards - Set Them

In an industry full of dropped balls and broken promises, **you get to be the exception.**

You get to be the one who:
- Shows up on time.
- Communicates clearly.
- Prices honestly.
- Delivers consistently.
- Follows through when others fade.

You become the standard by which others are measured - not because you're the loudest, but because you're the most reliable.

Let me give you an example:
In my previous business, I worked in an industry notorious for broken promises - building and renovation. Builders would show up late (if at all), quote one thing and charge another, start strong and disappear halfway through. So, I made a decision:

I would be different.

I priced in the "unseen" from the beginning. I warned clients of any rare potential unknowns - pipes behind walls, unexpected electrics, odd historical quirks - and if it ever arose, we had already discussed how it would be handled.

No surprises. No stress.

Clients came back again and again, not because I was the cheapest - I wasn't. But because they could go on holiday while I handled everything and return to exactly what I said I'd deliver.

That's the power of trust.

When You're Paid What You're Worth, You Can Show Up Fully
Let's be honest: the reason many people don't deliver with excellence is because they don't feel valued. They've dropped their price out of fear. They've said yes to clients who don't respect the process. And deep down, they're resentful.

Here's the pattern:
Undervaluing your offer leads to underperforming delivery.
Not always intentionally - but energetically.

So, value yourself enough to:
• Set a price that reflects the full power of what you offer.
• Work with clients who are a match for that standard.
• Deliver at 10 out of 10… because you were paid at 10 out of 10.

That's what real over-delivery looks like - not extras from insecurity, but excellence from alignment.

My Final Word: Exceed Expectations by Being the Real Deal
People can buy templates and tips from anywhere.
What they can't buy is your integrity.

So instead of hiding behind the cliché of "under-promise and over-deliver," lead with a new standard:

"I promise what's real. I price it fairly.
I deliver it faithfully. And I show up with everything I've got."

Do that - and not only will your clients get results...
They'll talk about you.
Refer you.
Respect you.
And return to you - not because of the price...
But because of the peace of mind you provide.

Excellent!

Let's complete the C.A.R.E.S. framework with the final piece:

Strengthen & Nurture Your Community
Long after the invoice is paid and the project is delivered, there's one thing that will continue to generate value for your business: your community. Your community isn't just your customer list or social media followers. It's the people who feel connected to your mission, your message, and your method. It's your past clients, your current clients, and even your potential future clients who are quietly watching how you show up in the world.

The question is - *are you nurturing them? Or are you ignoring them until you need something?*

Strong communities are built on relationships, not transactions. They grow when you:

- **Check** in without an agenda.
- **Celebrate wins** alongside your clients, even if you're not directly involved.
- **Offer value freely** - through content, advice, insights, or introductions.
- **Include them in your journey,** sharing behind-the-scenes moments and lessons learned.
- **Give them a voice,** asking for feedback and making them feel heard.

People want to belong. They want to feel like they're part of something bigger than a purchase. They want to be seen as partners in your journey, not just numbers in a spreadsheet. This kind of connection doesn't happen overnight. It's cultivated over time, through consistent care, generous communication, and genuine curiosity. But when you do it well, your community becomes your **greatest asset**.

They'll become your advocates.
Your collaborators.
Your referral engine.

In short, your community becomes your legacy. So, whether it's through a private group, a regular newsletter, quarterly check-ins, or just the occasional handwritten note; stay close to your people. Because in a noisy, distracted world, the businesses that thrive are the ones that stay human, stay connected, and stay committed to serving long after the sale.

With that, the C.A.R.E.S. framework is complete. But before we close out this book, let's take a moment to tie it all together and leave you with a powerful conclusion that will move you into action.

When you choose to serve with consistency, heart, and intention, success doesn't have to be hunted, it's drawn to you. Every time you Continue the Journey, you're telling your clients they matter beyond the transaction. When you Actively Listen, you create space for trust to grow. When you Resolve Issues Quickly, you show integrity in action. When you Exceed Expectations, you build a reputation that opens doors you never imagined. And when you Strengthen and Nurture Your Community, you build a legacy far beyond a single sale.

C.A.R.E.S. is not just a method, it's a movement. A way of doing business that puts people first and transforms customers into lifelong advocates. If you've ever wondered how to stand out in a crowded marketplace, this is it. Be the business that remembers birthdays. Be the voice that follows up with care. Be the experience that over-delivers every single time, because in a world full of noise, the most magnetic force of all is genuine service.

Let this chapter be your reminder that the sale is never the finish line, it's just the beginning of a deeper journey. One where trust is built, transformation happens, and everybody wins.

Now, let's turn the page and step into the conclusion, because this isn't the end. It's the start of something extraordinary.

*In a world of A.I pick up the phone &
let people hear your humanness*

*Make sure you take time out from your phone & connect
to nature if you want to turn up for your customer*

marcus
elwell
SALES MINDSET TRANSFORMATION

Let's connect on
social media

CONCLUSION

If you've made it here, then congratulations, because that means you've not only committed to reading this book, but you've also opened yourself up to a new way of being. A way of seeing sales not as a dirty word or a manipulative practice, but as an act of service. An opportunity to create connection, shift lives, and align with your highest potential. Throughout this book, I've worked to help you shift your mindset, reframe what a salesperson is, and redefine what selling really means. Sales isn't about convincing, it's about connecting. It's not about closing deals, it's about opening relationships. And most of all, it's not about pushing, it's about serving. By implementing the clear, heart-led structures and strategies I've shared, daily practices, powerful questioning frameworks, mindset shifts, authentic follow-ups, you are becoming the version of yourself you were always destined to be.

The version of you who dreamed boldly before life told you to shrink. The version of you who knows deep down that there's greatness within, waiting to be activated.

I've done the work. I've walked through the fire, rewired my beliefs, rebuilt businesses from nothing, and helped others do the same. And here's what I know with every cell of my being: **if you put in the work, this changes everything.**

But make no mistake, this is work. This isn't a magic formula or a shortcut to success. It's about doing the inner work, the heart work, and the service work. If you commit to the principles in this book for 7 days, then 21, then 90... you will reprogram your habits, your patterns, your mindset, and ultimately your results.

You'll show up differently. You'll speak with more conviction. You'll sell from a place of love and alignment. You'll attract opportunities without chasing. And most importantly, you'll build a business, or a career, that doesn't just make money but makes a difference.

When you sell from the heart, when you truly care about the outcome for the person in front of you, you create a ripple of impact that goes far beyond what you see. Because when you lead with service, **everybody wins.**

That's when the magic happens: abundance of clients, abundance of income, abundance of joy. It's all connected. The more you align with your true self and serve from that place, the more magnetic and successful you become, not just in business, but in life.

So, here's my final ask: implement what you've learned. Don't let this book sit on a shelf. Use it. Live it. Become the person your younger self always dreamed of.

And when you do, come find me. Share your story. Post your results. Message me on social media. Let me know how this work has changed your world, because I believe it will. And I can't wait to celebrate your success.

Until then - go out there, serve boldly, sell with heart, and remember in the world you're building, everybody wins.

BBC as inspirational speaker sharing my story of hope & resilience & raising awareness for brain tumour.

ACKNOWLEDGEMENT

First and foremost, I want to thank my family, who have stood by me step by step through every trial and tribulation. To my mum and dad - your unwavering love and support have been humbling, to say the least. You never judged, only supported, and helped me get through life's toughest moments.

To my sister Tamar, my brother-in-law Phil, my brother Matt, and my sister-in-law Carrie you've all played an instrumental role in holding me up when life tried to knock me down. And to all their children - thank you. We've all been through a lot, especially over these past four years, which I speak about in this book. Your support has carried me.
This book is dedicated to all of you.

My three greatest inspirations Millie, Noah, and Gracie my beautiful children. You are the reason I strive to be the best version of myself every single day. This book is for you too. I want you to know that no matter what life throws at you, no matter how hard or overwhelming it may seem you will overcome. Nothing lasts forever. No pain, no situation, no hardship is permanent. Everything passes, and if you can breathe through those hard moments and choose to believe, really believe that you have the power to shape your own destiny, then your life will never be the same.

The Creator - the Lord, the universe, the higher intelligence - did not design us for mediocrity. Yes, life was designed with challenges in it, but we were given the power of choice. You can become whoever you choose to be, at any time, no matter your past. If you can get your mind right, your body right, your thoughts aligned, you can thrive. Not just survive. Thrive.

To my friends who've stood by me - especially in the past few years - you know who you are. Paul, Stewart, Dave, Rich - thank you. You were instrumental in my healing and in becoming the man I am today. The laughter, the love, the adventures (and the ones we're about to have. Dolomites, here we come!) have meant the world to me. You've been my rock. Thank you to my oldest friends Chinas Scott who has been solid through my journey & Jason who has supported me throughout my health journey - doing Hyrox with me, triathlons and many more - your support is invaluable.

A special Mention to my oldest best friend Stu who not only looks like the rock with hair but has been my rock.

To Andy Harrington - thank you. When I joined your journey two years ago, you helped me see what I'd forgotten in myself. You believed in me. You pushed me. You showed me another way to live and what life could truly be like. I'm grateful for your guidance and mentorship.

To everyone reading this book - go all in on your life. Show up. Be bold. Be honest with yourself. Align your heart with your words, your work, and your relationships. Whether in sales or in life, when you move from a place of purpose and passion, you will see powerful change.
And finally, to my girlfriend Charlotte - thank you. You showed me what love is truly supposed to look like. ♡

Your love, your kindness, your support... they've been a healing I didn't even know I needed. I'm so grateful you came into my life and that I get to walk this path with you.

*My inspiration to get better my kids
Millie, Noah & Gracie*

*My beautiful girlfriend & rock
throughout my journey Charlotte*

Completed wolf run with kids

National Three Peak Challenge with my ride or dies that have been the back bone to my success over these last few years & my best friends Paul, Witham, David, Sidley & my main man Stuart, peers who have been my rock & with me every step of the way.

ABOUT THE AUTHOR

Marcus Elwell is the dynamic co-founder of The Heart of the Sale, a transformational sales and mindset company helping entrepreneurs and sales teams sell with authenticity, empathy, and impact. With over 25 years of experience building businesses from the ground up, Marcus has successfully scaled two companies to seven figures, one in the retail industry and another in property development, both alongside his family, navigating the incredible highs and inevitable challenges that come with entrepreneurship. But Marcus's true journey is as much internal as it is external. Behind the business success is a man who's walked through fire, personally, emotionally, and spiritually. Having faced and overcome financial collapse, health scares, and dark nights of the soul, Marcus has emerged with a renewed mission: to help others live and lead from their most powerful, authentic self.

At the heart of his message is a simple but revolutionary truth: When you change the way you think, the things you think about change.
This isn't just theory for Marcus, it's lived experience. Through deep inner work, Marcus has transformed his mind, body, soul, and bank balance. His unique sales methodology integrates human psychology, emotional intelligence, neuroscience, and practical strategy to help clients not only improve their conversion rates but elevate their entire way of being. Marcus believes that sales is not about pressure, it's about purpose. Not about sleaze, it's about service. And not about manipulation, it's about meaningful human connection.

Marcus has trained teams and individuals across industries, from property firms and CBD companies to manufacturing, media, accounting, coaching, and wellness brands. His signature method has helped clients double their close rates, raise their prices with confidence, and lead with heart, not hustle. His clients include respected leaders and brands such as Rob Moore's property team, Kevin Wright, and Jamie Stewart from the Circle Network. Whether working with solo entrepreneurs or entire sales teams, Marcus consistently helps people move from fear to flow, and from stuck to sold, with integrity. He is also a passionate advocate for mental wellbeing and human potential. Having experienced near-death moments that reshaped his perspective, Marcus now lives with one mission: to ensure no human being reaches the end of their life wondering "what if?" He champions mindset shifts that prevent burnout, breakdown, and wasted potential, empowering people to reclaim their worth, their voice, and their path.

Marcus is also deeply committed to charitable causes. He's currently raising funds for brain tumour research and training for a mini–Iron Man, the London Marathon, and a trek across the Arctic Circle—all to prove that hope, healing, and strength are always possible, no matter how broken you may feel. When he's not speaking, training, or coaching, Marcus shares his message through his book, events, and online content. His passion is contagious, his methods are proven, and his heart is rooted in service.

"Sales," Marcus says, "isn't just what you do—it's who you are. And when you become aligned with your truth, sales become a natural extension of your purpose."

marcus
elwell

SALES MINDSET TRANSFORMATION

www.ingramcontent.com/pod-product-compliance
Lightning Source LLC
Chambersburg PA
CBHW071235210326
41597CB00016B/2062